From Zero to Eleven Plus: English
Self-tutor study guide for Upper Primary, Lower Secondary and E

From Zero to Eleven Plus: English offers shortcuts to writing well for upper primar entrance tests. It takes the student on a journey through ambitious vocabulary, s description to an exploration of narrative, information and persuasive text. It provid and stimulating tasks to advance the learning. The comprehensions cover three mode ... retrieval, inference and stylistic. Useful vocabulary lists combine adjectives with nouns, and verbs with adverbs. What makes good writing checklists provide essential prompts to planning, creating and developing text. A final section provides booster projects that students may wish to tackle first, if required.

From Zero to Eleven Plus: English is written by experienced practitioners, who have an exemplary record for making a positive difference to exam grades and to gaining a place at top secondary schools. For less than the cost of one hour's tutoring, it supports outstanding achievement.

Contents

Ambitious vocabulary and poetry 2

Poetry: Identifying poetic devices, with comprehension and answers 3

Investigating punctuation, with *In Control* – Part One 5

Sentence types 6

Upgrading text 7

Descriptive text: getting started 8

Descriptive text: places, people, objects and events 9

Features of narrative genre: comedy, ghost, social realism, mystery, science fiction and fantasy 12

Narrative genre montage 13

How to write an entertaining short story 14

Ghost narratives: *The Castle* and *The Lion Hunter*, with planning prompts 17

Social realism and mystery narrative: *The Library Thief*, with planning prompts 20

Science fiction narrative: *In Control* – Part Two, with planning prompts 22

Fantasy narrative: *Just* – with analysis, planning prompts, comprehension and answers 24

Formal letter writing 28

Play script 29

Features of recounts, including diary writing 30

Autobiographical text: *The Autobiography of the Major Oak* 31

Report writing: *The Battle of Dunkirk*, with comprehension and answers 32

Newspaper report writing: *The Miracle of Dunkirk* 34

Witness report writing 35

Persuasive writing: adverts, two-sided arguments and persuasive leaflets 36

Explanation text 38

Invitations and instructions 39

Useful vocabulary: How? Verbs and corresponding adverbs: to describe movement, speaking, seeing, eating and meeting 40

Useful vocabulary: What? Adjectives: to describe nouns for people, creatures, cityscapes, landscapes, seascapes, seasons and the weather 41

What makes good writing checklists 42

Oliver Island: Booster projects to support the understanding of what makes good writing 47

ISBN: 978-0-9568427-0-1
First Edition – March 2011
Copyright © 2011 by Caroline Brice
Published by Andrew Crisp
3 Godson Road, CR0 4LT, UK
Tel: +44 (0)20 8686 9796
Email: books@zerotoelevenplus.co.uk
Web: www.zerotoelevenplus.co.uk
Editors: Caroline Brice and Amy Brice

From Zero to Eleven Plus: Mathematics and *From Zero to Eleven Plus: Verbal Reasoning* are also available. **£14.99**
For more information, please visit **www.zerotoelevenplus.co.uk**

Ambitious vocabulary and poetry

Poetry is a great way to say more with less and therefore requires the use of the optimum word for expression. In splitting ambitious vocabulary into four columns of: adjectives, nouns, adverbs and verbs, it is possible to construct four succinct lines that are then completed with one of the whole location lines provided, as shown in the sample stanzas below. Use these words and lines to invent poetry before creating your own bank of words and lines for your own original poetry.

Adjectives	Nouns	Adverbs	Verbs
Galloping	waves	wearily	guarding
Arrogant	cows	menacingly	dominating
Crooked	rocks	explosively	watching
Malicious	winds	collectively	provoking
Whistling	smiles	foolishly	persuading
Huddled	warriors	curiously	tormenting
Devious	wizards	ferociously	attacking
Rugged	trees	religiously	challenging
Obstinate	words	haphazardly	embracing
Ramshackle	men	fearfully	ridiculing
Ancient	clouds	angrily	mimicking
Pretentious	holes	frantically	intimidating

The haunted house on the stoic hill.
The uncultivated creatures of the forbidden forest.
The mocking parrots of Whispering Wood.
The crunchy gravel of the solemn cemetery.
The roaming cats of St Grey's Peak.
The terrified passengers on the 9.45 flight to the moon.
The roaring crowds of the dark city.
The aggressive bats of the solitary castle.
The angry waves of the threatening ocean.
The tickling grass of Daffodil Valley.
The confused crowd of Wild Geese Marsh.
The magical stones of the enchanted island.

Sample:

Galloping waves ferociously attacking
Rugged rocks religiously guarding
Crooked trees curiously watching
Malicious clouds explosively challenging
The mocking parrots of Whispering Wood.

Obstinate winds collectively tormenting
Huddled warriors wearily provoking
Whistling wizards haphazardly mimicking
Ancient men foolishly embracing
The magical stones of the enchanted island.

Poetry: Identifying poetic devices and comprehension

Boots

Uniform marching in gallant company
Proudly paraded, young and chatty
Bold, black boots like ants in a line
Swallowed by the mumbling plane
An oncoming storm with tears of rain
Ready or not the boots can't hide
Running and muddied
Torn and bloodied
Older than their years, scarred boots lose ground
In treacherous explosive terrain, footwear fall battered
One left boot, alone and shattered
Lost in action.

The Pier

Grumpy old pier on a dangerous dark night
Fleetingly illuminated by lightning – knives slicing the sky
Exhausted, bruised and aching
Two gates screech open like a dying animal
On to this graveyard of decaying planks
To the abandoned fairground, not wanted.
The hysterical haunted house howls
Melancholically in the bullying wind
Frightening the decomposing carousel horses
With their long, cold and unfriendly stares
Speared by poles, sobbing in the impetuous rain
Attacked by the malicious thrashing, clashing, smashing, whooshing waves
Which pelt them with thunderous smacks of racing ice water
And spiteful sharp stones
Skimming like a tumbling clown as if in fun to the Comedy House
But the sign says 'closed'.

COMPREHENSION QUESTIONS – BOOTS

1. List one adjective that describes the boot before battle and another adjective that describes the boot during battle that demonstrates the change to the boot. (Retrieval)

2. Who is wearing the boots? (Inference)

3. What is the 'oncoming storm' a metaphor for? (Stylistic)

COMPREHENSION QUESTIONS – THE PIER

1. What is 'sobbing in the rain'? (Retrieval)

2. Why does it fit the poem to say that the Comedy House is 'closed'? (Inference)

3. Name two things that are personified and list the words that personify them. (Stylistic)

TASK:

Annotate each poem to show you can identify poetic devices, such as: alliteration, rhythm and onomatopoeia (*buzzing, busy bees*), repetition (*lurking with intent, malicious intent in the darkest of darkest shadows*), personification (*the angry sea spat spiteful stones at the devastated beach*), similes (*as dark as coal or coal-dark*), metaphors (*the willow tree was an old lady*), comparable theme (*through the cemetery-like gates, past the dying trees to the house that looked ghostly in the deathly-grey fog*), rhyme (*the clock out of time, with a discordant chime*).

Now, use poetic devices to write your own poem entitled either:

❑ Haunted House

❑ Audience

❑ Mirror

❑ The Journey

❑ The Ocean

Comprehension answers – Boots

1. Adjectives that describe the boot before battle that will later contrast with the boot during war are: *young*, *chatty* and *bold*. Adjectives that describe the boot during battle that demonstrate the change to the boot are: *muddied*, *torn*, *bloodied*, *scarred* and *battered*.

2. A soldier wears the boots.

3. 'Oncoming storm' is a metaphor for the forthcoming battle.

Comprehension answers – The Pier

1. The carousel horses are 'sobbing in the rain'.

2. It fits the poem to say that the Comedy House is 'closed' because there is no fun on the pier anymore. Or, because the pier is 'closed' for business. Or, this question can be interpreted as a stylistic question and 'closed' fits the poem as it effectively ends it.

3. The poem uses personification with reference to the: pier (*grumpy*), gates (*screech*), haunted house (*hysterical howls*), wind (*bullying*), carousel horses (*sobbing*), waves (*malicious and smacks*) and stones (*spiteful*).

Investigating punctuation

A good way to understand punctuation is to read correctly punctuated text and work out the purpose of each type of punctuation.

In Control – Part One

The chattering city was instantly disturbingly quiet. An unexpected, ominous darkness brought the car-cramped streets to a halt. Floyd, who had been following the cracks on the uneven pavement, stopped (one foot stuck unnaturally behind the other in a line). The young boy instinctively looked upwards; his mother did too. The sky was a midnight-black, but it wasn't nighttime. Strangely, the space around the top of two neighbouring, tall office blocks seemed to be moving. The bustling solid dark blanket suddenly broke into black commas in the afternoon sky as chinks of light broke through. Floyd's mum gasped as the dark punctuation rapidly increased in size. Millions of flying creatures were heading in their direction and the clattering of their wings, striking their armoured bodies, was now audible and terrifying. The menacing army frontline was just seconds away, with several layers of crunchy, clicking reinforcements behind them.

Floyd and his mum were knocked to the ground as the heavy swarm bombarded them – this was the first of the 'flying commas' attacks. A piercing scream cut through the city: it was a scream that only the very desperate can make because when Floyd's mum stood back up, her son was not there! "Where is my son?" she shrieked at all the shocked, immobile onlookers.

One woman managed to point at the sky. "The creatures took your son," she uttered, incredulously.

Floyd's mum followed the gaze of the large audience – there in the sky were two legs dangling from a massive full stop that was flying away. "Fight Floyd," she screamed, helplessly.

She then began a hopeless chase below the clattering ball, but she couldn't keep up. She watched the large black mass head away from the city towards the thirsty desert, where, without water, a young boy would not survive for very long…

INVESTIGATION INTO PUNCTUATION TASK:

Highlight the punctuation in the above Science Fiction text, checking its purpose with the punctuation definitions. Then, read an exciting book and work out why each type of punctuation is used.
Apply correct punctuation in your own work.

❑ A sentence begins with a capital and ends with a **full stop**, **question mark**, **exclamation mark**, **end speech mark** or **ellipses**.

❑ **Brackets** involve clarifying information or an aside comment.

❑ **Hyphens** are used when one word links to another as a shortened simile (midnight-black), to avoid multiple letters connecting (co-ordinate), with some prefixes and suffixes (self-sufficient), to form compound words and with initial letters (U-turn).

❑ A **semi-colon** links two sentences that can join up and so is instead of a conjunction.

❑ An **apostrophe** is used to indicate possession as mum belongs to Floyd (Floyd's mum) or for a contraction, such as couldn't.

❑ A **colon** is used for definition via a list, summary or quote.

❑ **Commas** are used in a list instead of and, before a conjunction, to add subordinate information and before final speech marks when a question mark or an exclamation mark are not used before the speech verb.

❑ **Speech marks** are used around what is directly spoken. A new paragraph is given to a new speaker.

❑ A **dash** is used for explanation with extra information.

❑ **Single quotation marks** are used for indirect quotes, quotes within quotes and new vocabulary.

❑ **Ellipses** are used to indicate missing words or that more is to come.

Sentence types

A **simple sentence**, that is an *independent clause*, usually contains a subject and a predicate (which tells us something about the subject) and it expresses a complete thought. On occasion, authors include a one-word sentence to express an instruction, emotion or description. Sentences can end in five different ways, with a: full stop, question mark, an exclamation mark, closing speech mark or ellipses.

Sam put on the strange jacket. It fitted perfectly.

A **compound sentence** contains two *independent clauses* joined by a co-ordinating conjunction (*for, and, but, or, yet, so*) or a semi-colon that acts as the conjunction.

Anya looked at him and then she burst into giggles. Grumpily, Sam took off the jacket, but it was too late; he was under the magician's power.

A **complex sentence** has an *independent clause* joined by one or more *dependent (subordinate) clauses*. A complex sentence may have a subordinator such as *because, if, since, after, although, whenever* or *when* or a relative pronoun (or implied relative pronoun) such as *that, who, whose* or *which*. It is useful to note that commas are used after or around a subordinate clause.

The magician, (who was) hidden by some trees, made Sam dance involuntarily. After his eccentric boogie, the children walked home not speaking.

It is relatively easy to convert **simple** to **compound sentences** as this involves joining two independent clauses that go together, with a co-ordinating conjunction.

Sam was embarrassed. His strange dance had made him look ridiculous.

Sam was embarrassed for his strange dance had made him look ridiculous.

Complex sentences are useful for adding further information without repeating the subject.

Anya, who was good at dancing, could not believe her eyes!

or   *Biting her lip for distraction, Anya could not trust herself to speak about it without dissolving into further fits of laughter.*

It is important to be able to use all three types of sentences; reading a series of just one type of sentence can be very laborious. More accomplished writing uses different sentence types for various reasons, such as the use of simple, short sentences amongst longer sentences for dramatic effect. Also, being able to give more information about the same subject through compound and complex sentences avoids the 'staccato' effect. Compound-complex sentences include two main clauses and a sub-ordinate clause.

TASK:

Read some entertaining chapter books or exciting short stories, identify sentence types and consider the effect they have on the reader in order that you can write with increasing sophistication.

Upgrading text

Simple sentences have a purpose. For example, they can be good for dramatic effect amongst longer sentences and for providing clear instructions. Therefore, it is important to look at whole text when upgrading it and to consider the purpose of the writing. However, to bring together the work on ambitious, optimum vocabulary (including adjectives and adverbs) and the learning about sentences, basic sentences are provided below for upgrading.

The man walked up the hill to a cottage.	Heavy, crisp footsteps showed purposeful, though cautious, progress up the snowy coat of the track, as the young man nervously approached the tormented cottage on the hill.
He remembered the building's past.	
He opened the door.	
It was dark inside.	
A noise came from upstairs.	

Shelley walked along the beach.	
The beach was deserted.	
She momentarily watched the sea.	
She found a bottle with a message in it.	
She was surprised by the message.	

Descriptive text: success criteria

In this section, we are going to consider success criteria for writing description before describing a place, a character, an object or an event or a combination of these.

Description should entertain and convey a vivid picture of what is described. It is important to have a clear image of what you are describing. Features that enhance description include:

❑ Ambitious and relevant vocabulary, including adjectives and adverbs (see pages 40 and 41).

❑ Describing more than what can be seen. For example, what can be heard? What can be smelt? How does the character/narrator feel?

❑ Poetic language to bring text to life and convey a strong picture through clever comparisons, using similes, metaphors, personification and complimentary themes, such as death. Alliteration, onomatopoeia, repetition and rhythm can give a sound to the writing that perhaps even suggests what is being described.

❑ Perceptive, interesting detail and insightful comments about what we describe (including imperfections), that make the reader believe they know exactly what we are describing and that we must have experienced what we describe.

❑ Being creative in how we convey the whole picture. For example, a torch beam, character, animal or insect moving around a place can enable a seemingly natural flow of description, while also showing cause and effect by using more than one verb in a sentence. (For example: The neglected stone steps *crumbled* as he *mounted* them.) An acceptable order of description can also be created if the writer describes a set of images that a movie camera might capture as it moves along the scene.

❑ Building up suspense, which can be done through vocabulary, sensory description, weather, lighting, dramatic statements made through short sentences amongst longer sentences, the addition of a curious object, person or event, an expression of feelings from a likeable character, with questions, vocabulary and phrases that convey a particular mood, with the powerful anticipation of an enemy, who may cause great danger within a remote setting and the use of cliff-hangers with possibly a race against time.

❑ Giving the subject something extra, like an unexpected feature or some history, rumour, or character viewpoint with an implication of narrative, perhaps with a sense of the narrator's thoughts.

Description: getting started

1) Get an image of what you are describing in your head and sketch it so you know if you have enough of an image to describe. Alternatively, use a photograph or better still have what you are describing in front of you.

2) Add something to what you describe that will give you a chance to interest the reader by thinking beyond the moment you are describing. In the description below, I have added an undelivered letter to the scene.

3) List the nouns from top to bottom or side to side of your picture, so you are able to logically progress with your description. Around the nouns, add description with enough detail, action and necessary links to other text. My nouns are: sky, office blocks, clock tower, people, letter, pavement and traffic.

4) List the success criteria that you decide make this genre of writing particularly effective. In this case my success criteria is to: use ambitious vocabulary (relevant and interesting adjectives, verbs and adverbs), describe from more than just sight, use poetic devices and include something unusual into the scene. I must also bear in mind my overall aim: to convey a vivid impression of the town, with a composition that flows and entertains.

Nouns	Description, with enough detail, action and any necessary links to other text
sky	*The threatening grey sky darkened the concrete slabs of office blocks.*
office blocks	*These eyesores dominated the town.*
clock tower	*Out of place, the intricately decorated clock tower proudly boasted the time.*
people	*Nine-to-five people scurried briskly past this monument, like ants in a line, ignoring its surreal floral beauty and*
letter and pavement	*the important letter (in a carefully handwritten envelope) that had been carelessly dropped on the uneven pavement nearby. A burst of icy-cold rain, that made the unprepared pedestrians shiver, also made the envelope instantly anonymous. So, Lucy James would not know she was offered the office job, where she would have met the man she would have married. She would not have the two children she would have had, one of whom would have made an important scientific discovery that would have saved mankind!*
clock tower and traffic	*The clock tower chimed nine o'clock with haughty indifference, sending pigeons off in frantic, wing-smacking flight, while smoking, tooting, aggressively revving traffic stood unable to splash the pedestrians, thanks to the bossy red light.*

The threatening grey sky darkened the concrete slabs of office blocks. These eyesores dominated the town. Out of place, the intricately decorated clock tower proudly boasted the time. Nine-to-five people scurried briskly past this monument, like ants in a line, ignoring its surreal floral beauty and the important letter (in a carefully handwritten envelope) that had been carelessly dropped on the uneven pavement nearby. A burst of icy-cold rain, that made the unprepared pedestrians shiver, also made the envelope instantly anonymous. So, Lucy James would not know she was offered the office job, where she would have met the man she would have married. She would not have the two children she would have had, one of whom would have made an important scientific discovery that would have saved mankind! The clock tower chimed nine o'clock with haughty indifference, sending pigeons off in frantic, wing-smacking flight, while smoking, tooting, aggressively revving traffic stood unable to splash the pedestrians, thanks to the bossy red light.

5) Evaluate your writing to the success criteria as a way to develop your writing as you go along.

Descriptive text: places

A Room with No Way Out – version one

The room was dark, though there was a bit of light from the moon. The door handle had come off. A red puddle was on the floor. It was blood. There was a noise upstairs. I was scared. Footsteps came closer. I was more scared. I thought I would die.

A Room with No Way Out – version two

Had I just made a terrible mistake?

Rain tapped urgently against the glass pane, which was ferociously guarded by substantial, vertical metal bars. The door had swung closed with a hostile, though inexplicable, gust and the handle, having given way, was now clasped in my hand and dangled by my thigh. Useless! A dark cockroach scratched across the dusty, dusk-grey floor, another trespasser taking shelter.

The damp smell of deterioration dominated the remaining air as I tried not to hyperventilate. But, a sudden bolt of lightning illuminated a dark red puddle on the stark floorboards, meeting my new boots with stickiness. No! My excessive breathing accompanied the exchange of my gaze from below to above. Drip! My face was spitefully spotted with thick drops of…blood. I let out a fearful screech, the kind that is someone's last. Intimidating silence! Not even the cockroach could now be seen or heard. Briefly scared that no one would hear me, I was swiftly heart haltingly terrified, as I heard heavy footsteps suddenly react and burst into life across the floor above me. I froze to the spot, an animal trapped.

Down the stairs, my destiny hastily approached, as the door was swung open on my unforgiving trap.

Distant scratching down the hallway confirmed that the cockroach had managed to escape!

Descriptive text: people

Lady Romilly

Lady Romilly smells like a meadow of daisies and sounds posh when she talks because she stresses her consonants and she says crazy things like, "How dare people make me feel guilty by being so poor!" Actually, to be honest, I don't think she is really a lady because she lives next door to my Mum and I, and we're not rich.

"If she's a lady, I'm the Queen," my Mum says, but we politely smile at her anyway.

Lady Romilly has straight, granite-grey hair that provides a neat outline to her thin face that is lined like an overused map that has always been incorrectly folded. She wears silver-rimmed, round glasses that are peculiarly perched further down her bony nose than seems normal or useful and her narrow, solemn lips wear a red lipstick that she probably wore in her twenties and which contrasts starkly with her tissue paper-pale skin.

"I'm off to the Palace," she shouts.

"She's off to Palace Bingo!" says my Mum, but we wave to her, as she painfully teeters up the short path and slowly twists and lowers her fatigued and slightly stooping body into the back of the mini cab, pulling her stoic walking stick behind her. An arthritic hand weakly pulls the stubborn car door closed.

She now wears a counterfeit smile, with her teeth pushing out her lips as she sticks up her nose and sits back, pretending she is in a comfortable limousine.

TASK:

Using the success criteria for descriptive writing on page 7, mark the passage, 'Lady Romilly'. Then, with reference to the success criteria, describe a real or imaginary person or character, before editing and developing your work from your own marking:

❑ Lady Romilly   ❑ My Imaginary Friend   ❑ Mr Jones

❑ My Favourite Person   ❑ The Beast   ❑ Grumpy Joe

Descriptive text: objects

Use the success criteria, at the beginning of this section, to mark the passage, 'A Pencil'.

Remember: similes can be shortened, so 'white as a lily' can become 'lily-white'. Also, a seemingly ordinary object can be given a history and be part of a narrative. A comparison can be continued into a theme; in this description, features of the pencil are related to 'predator', 'wasp' and 'sting'.

A Pencil

Light captures the top, shiny plane of my yellow and black, wasp pencil. It is not perfectly flat as someone (not me) has bitten into the end of it and left a set of predator bite marks, just past the little pink, graphite-smudged rubber that is partly imprisoned by a fine, slither of non-precious metal, which has a set of two pairs of parallel grooves and two tiny holes that tightly unite the wood of the pencil and the rubber. The narrow hexagonal prism is easy to grip and two fingers and a thumb slide towards the end, which narrows to a menacingly sharp, school uniform-grey point, with a sting that is ready to attack the lily-white paper.

As the Mathematics lesson begins, I look around to work out who bit my pencil. Connor Morris, hiding behind his spider-black hair, glances around suspiciously. He is my main suspect!

TASK:

With reference to the success criteria on page 7, describe one of the following objects, before editing and developing your work from your own marking:

❑ A Pencil   ❑ The Old Box   ❑ My Diary

❑ A Boot   ❑ The Armchair   ❑ The Door

Descriptive text: events

Describing an event or a series of events can also be categorised under recount such as autobiographical writing. It is a good mechanism for portraying character. Sometimes present tense is used which gives a sense that the event is happening contemporaneously.

Meal Time

When the smoke alarm goes off in our house, we all know Mum is about to serve up food! "Supper," she shouts, unnecessarily.

Toby, Bluebell and I race downstairs vying for first place (Toby usually wins). We sit in our set places, around a perfectly square wooden table, as our stressed mum presents the food on the pretty floral plates (that were Grandma's) – chips, peas and burnt pie – yum! Bluebell reaches for the ketchup and sends Toby's juice over him. She then squirts the ketchup down her faded school sweatshirt, as Toby elbows her, while I sit demurely eating the food, as if we are in a posh restaurant. "Did you have a nice day at work, Mum?" I ask, to distract her from the ensuing battle of blame between my little brother and sister.

My Mum visibly relaxes and smiles. "It was okay," she answers. "How was your day?"

The question is for me, but Toby stops the war and answers. "Someone threw a book at someone else and it hit Mrs Marco" (Mrs Marco is Toby's long suffering and unfortunate teacher).

My Mum looks at Toby. "Did you throw the book?" she asks, with a neutral tone.

"Me?" asks Toby, guiltily, as he puts up his eyebrows in fake surprise at such an unfair suggestion.

"He did it!" states Bluebell.

Toby's face changes to his pouting lips, narrowing eyes and tightening eyebrows' face as he suddenly realises he didn't need to say a thing.

TASK:

When describing an event, include the description of the main, interesting moments. Write it as you would say it. Use a short introduction to interest the reader and a short concluding statement to give it finality.

These titles might help you decide what to write about:

❑ Meal Time ❑ The Journey ❑ The Storm

❑ The time I was nervous ❑ A Memorable Day ❑ Mission

Features of narrative genre

Although there may be some crossover, each narrative genre is attached to a series of expectations. While developing as a writer, it is easier to create a successful story by applying the genre specifications.

Genre	Setting	Characters	Events	Style	Vocabulary
Comedy	Fits with other genre, but mostly contemporary, around a main setting like school or home.	A main, mostly amiable, character(s) with major flaws interacting with likeable characters with other strong characteristics.	A situation is built up that plays with the main character's major flaws so that the reader laughs at the absurd aspects of human behaviour, whilst the main character has a contrary intention to what actually happens.	Understanding of the character through their actions and speech. The reader is put into a position of knowing more than the flawed character.	Adjectives: *clumsy, arrogant* Verbs: *reddening, interfering* Adverbs: *haphazardly, boastfully*
Ghost	Remote, dark and stormy, sometimes an old, grand building.	Ghosts and the living or a ghost that the reader believes is a living character until a final revelation.	Eerie, other world events are experienced by a likeable character up to a final revelation. Ghosts may bring a living character into a previous, terrifying moment or the main character may be brought to a realisation they are a ghost!	Builds up suspense through eerie description, the asking of vexed questions, with short bursts of emotion or observation amongst longer sentences up to the final revelation.	Adjectives: *remote, stormy* Verbs: *crept, hesitated* Adverbs: *apprehensively, abruptly*
Social Realism	Realistic, sometimes a home or a school.	Main character set alongside other characters that either cause the social issues or support the character.	Main character succeeds in spite of all the challenges they are caused by their social situation.	Description of setting and events form the backdrop to the characters, strongly conveyed through their dialogue and behaviour, with the main character developing as the story progresses.	Adjectives: *dilapidated, scruffy* Verbs: *confessed, slurped* Adverbs: *nonchalantly, angrily*
Mystery	Realistic, crime scene.	Villain and character to solve the crime.	A main character works hard to solve the mystery about a crime committed. Clues are revealed as the action progresses, but some information is withheld as the solution is revealed at the end.	Can be narrated, with a suspicious, though confident tone, by the detective. Description and suspicious questions add to the feeling that all is not right.	Adjectives: *shadowy, murky* Verbs: *lurking, advanced* Adverbs: *suspiciously, emphatically*
Science Fiction	Futuristic, outer space or realistic (with invasion).	Possible futuristic villain/robot or alien and futuristic or 'real' hero or heroine.	Science and technology that is out of control or an invasion. The main character saves mankind from all danger.	Builds up suspense through danger that threatens mankind. Uses descriptive language to give picture of unknown.	Adjectives: *slimy, metallic* Verbs: *vibrated, programmed* Adverbs: *expertly, smoothly*
Fantasy	Imagined or realistic, possibly with a portal.	Fantasy villain and fantasy or 'real' conquering hero or heroine.	Adventure whereby hero has to save others perhaps by defeating a villain or by achieving their quest for a crucial item, while overcoming a series of dilemmas.	Description of fantastical setting, characters and invented vocabulary in fast pace, series of events.	Adjectives: *intimidating, diminutive* Verbs: *soared, croaked* Adverbs: *grumpily, swiftly*

Narrative genre montage

The Bus Journey: can you recognise the different genre?

The overcrowded bus reluctantly crept up the hill. I passed several standing passengers to sit on the only available seat, at the back of the bus and I soon understood why this seat had not been previously taken. A young freckled faced boy lent forward. "Goggle Eyes!" he shouted at the boy on the other side of me.

I looked to my left and observed a slightly older boy with glasses reading a book. Just opposite him, another boy, who appeared even younger than the freckled boy, joined in, "Geek, Danny's talking to you."

The boy with the book looked up at the last antagonist. After some hesitation, he calmly decided, "Neither of you are worth talking to."

This it turned out was a declaration of war as fists began to stray around me and I was very glad that when the bus next stopped, a woman in the corner at the back, next to the reader, stood up and said, "Come on you mongrels!"

I said nothing as she bashed into me with her eco-enemy, plastic shopping bags. I then said nothing as her two mean boys knocked into me to follow her. The reader remained. "Very sensible," I thought.

"Ay nutter," shouted the clumsy woman, as she turned before leaving the bus, "get yourself over 'ere now. I'm gonna burn that silly book when we get home. It's making you stupid!" The scorned boy shuffled off the bus, reluctantly, and there was peace.

I moved over to the window seat of the shopper and some of the people standing now advanced to the tired and saggy, warm seats.

The bus was plunged into sudden darkness as if we had just gone into a tunnel, away from the bright daylight and it screeched melancholically to a halt. I looked up into the sky and was shocked to see a grey circular mass bobbing above us, blocking the sun. The front bus door suddenly swung open and I could hear heavy, metal footsteps move on to the bus and as light once again invaded the vehicle, I could see a robot at the front, shaking his head when asked to show his identity. I looked up at the sky – just wispy clouds and the sun, now. How strange!

As the bus continued, a sudden scream from the lady opposite me sent every gaze on the bus (except the driver's) to the back. "Someone's stolen my purse," she screamed. "I thought I felt something in that darkness."

Everyone at the back of the bus looked at each other suspiciously, but finally every gaze focused on the heplar, the half human, half fox, who was sat next to her, because as everyone knows heplars are very sly creatures. He narrowed his eyes, in anger. "It wasn't me!" he shouted and nobody argued with him because heplars can also be extremely spiteful.

Suddenly, the bus screeched. "What now?" called an old lady, about half way up the bus.

"There was a lady in the road," shouted the driver, shocked.

Immediately I stood up and looked behind the bus. Nothing!

"That's the Lady of Trent Village," shouted the old lady. "Was she wearing a long white dress and white lace hat?"

"Yes," answered the driver.

"Well then don't worry yourself; she died an hundred years ago," said the old lady.

"How do you know that?" asked the driver.

"Because she was my sister!"

TASK:

Describe in a chosen narrative genre or in a montage of genre types:

- ❑ The Bus Journey
- ❑ A Strange Day
- ❑ Why I was late to school
- ❑ The Museum
- ❑ The Beach
- ❑ Someone's taken my jelly beans!

How to write an entertaining short story

The content of a short story – ideas

Generate ideas from a title for the content by deciding which genre of narrative is suggested by the title. Then ask: *who? where? when? what? why? how?* to stimulate ideas for the characters, setting and plot.

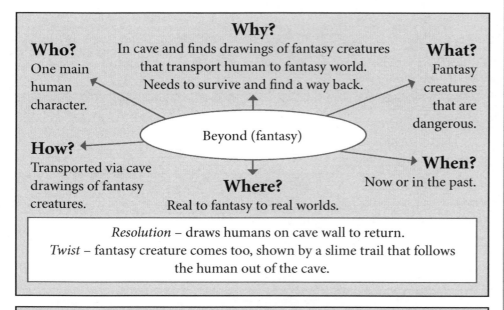

Why?
In cave and finds drawings of fantasy creatures that transport human to fantasy world. Needs to survive and find a way back.

Who?
One main human character.

What?
Fantasy creatures that are dangerous.

How?
Transported via cave drawings of fantasy creatures.

Beyond (fantasy)

Where?
Real to fantasy to real worlds.

When?
Now or in the past.

Resolution – draws humans on cave wall to return.
Twist – fantasy creature comes too, shown by a slime trail that follows the human out of the cave.

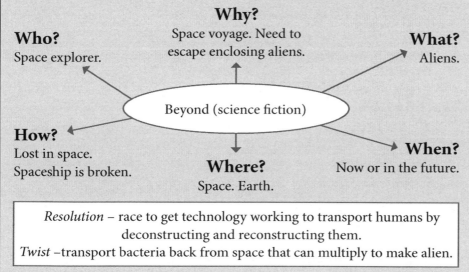

Why?
Space voyage. Need to escape enclosing aliens.

Who?
Space explorer.

What?
Aliens.

How?
Lost in space. Spaceship is broken.

Beyond (science fiction)

Where?
Space. Earth.

When?
Now or in the future.

Resolution – race to get technology working to transport humans by deconstructing and reconstructing them.
Twist –transport bacteria back from space that can multiply to make alien.

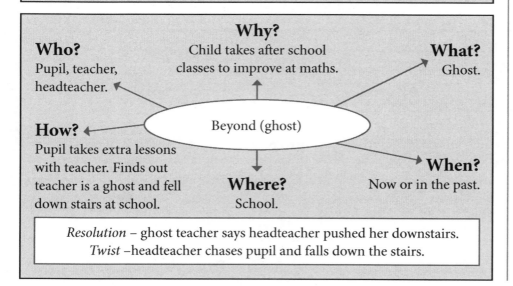

Why?
Child takes after school classes to improve at maths.

Who?
Pupil, teacher, headteacher.

What?
Ghost.

How?
Pupil takes extra lessons with teacher. Finds out teacher is a ghost and fell down stairs at school.

Beyond (ghost)

Where?
School.

When?
Now or in the past.

Resolution – ghost teacher says headteacher pushed her downstairs.
Twist –headteacher chases pupil and falls down the stairs.

The content of a short story – format

Paragraph one: The first sentence draws the reader in via interest in character, setting or action. The first paragraph introduces the main character, setting and sense of dilemma. It should end with a cliffhanger.

Middle paragraphs: An entertaining story requires an interesting idea for building the dilemma. The main character will be beset by exciting experiences that are well described and expressed. Paragraphs should end on cliff-hangers.

Resolution with a twist: The end should tie up the story with a twist. The end of a story might:

- ☐ End with the opening line
- ☐ Provide a surprise revelation about the main character or the other characters
- ☐ Tie up observations to solve a mystery
- ☐ Bring something from an alternative world into the 'real world'
- ☐ Provide a comic end, after a traumatic experience that shows all the trauma was unnecessary
- ☐ Use a clever idea to make a *vital narrow escape.*

The language of a short story

Start sentences variously

Connectives: *Immediately... After... Before... Finally... Suddenly... Meanwhile... Later... Then...*

Other adverbs: *Grumpily, (he stomped to the hostile house)... Wearily, (he wandered along the moonlit track)... Quietly, (she observed the mysterious box)... Slyly, (he concealed the strangely scribed parchment)... Carefully, (she hopped over the pavement cracks)...*

Verbs starting subordinate clauses: *Flaunting (his sword),... Pacing (a trail across),... Gasping (for breath),... Daunted (by the menacing hiss),... Grabbing (the beast by his horns),...*

Adjectives: *Animated (chatter filled the sumptuous chamber)... Unsettled, frightful (creatures eyed him suspiciously)...*

Nouns and pronouns: *Martha (stumbled down the anonymous alleyway)... She (looked suspiciously at...)*

Prepositions: *Above (the cranky city)... Inside (his special box)... Through (the forbidden forest)... Under (the rudimentary bridge)... Across (the star studded sky)... Beyond (the ankle-twisting, weather-etched track)...*

Use ambitious vocabulary

Adjectives: *agile, ancient, archaic, cavernous, cloudy, dilapidated, diminutive, discordant, distant, drab, dynamic, forbidden, harmonious, harsh, inferior, intimidating, luminous, milky, minute, murky, pleasant, repulsive, rusty, spotless, static, tranquil, unusual, voluminous.*

Speech verbs: *argued, bawled, boasted, challenged, croaked, demanded, grunted, insisted, joked, muttered, pleaded, stammered, reflected, reported, whispered.*

Verbs: *approached, celebrated, confused, crept, dominated, exploded, jostled, leapt, paused, posed, positioned, provoked, resisted, soared, struggled, tormented.*

Adverbs: *abruptly, aggressively, agitatedly, athletically, awkwardly, bashfully, carelessly, casually, cautiously, decisively, desperately, deviously, dismissively, earnestly, ecstatically, extravagantly, fancifully, fervently, feverishly, fiercely, frantically, frostily, generously, gracefully, greedily, hastily, incredulously, indifferently, jovially, maliciously, melancholically, menacingly, persuasively, strangely, swiftly, tentatively.*

Use poetic devices

Personification: The fog crept over the confused city... Darkness lingered down the alley... Tired shoes shuffled...

Similes: Lily-white, midnight-black, wrinkled as an old leather glove, scared as a cornered rabbit...

Metaphors: Morning was an energetic boy... Evening was a tired, old man... The tree was a stern general...

Build up suspense

Vocabulary: *strange, forbidding, intimidating, withered, ghostly, unnatural, precariously, grimly, volatile, ruthless...*

Sensory description: Monstrous dark shadows changed into the shape of a wild beast... An unusual scratching momentarily distracted her... Ice-cold water swept him into an uncontrollable spin... Heavy, purposeful footsteps approached... A cocktail of strange pungent smells emanated from the squalid room...

Dangerous setting: *stormy, remote, dark...*

Questions: What had left those deep scratch marks? If she screamed, who would hear her?

Cliffhangers: She was trapped! In this barren valley, there was nowhere to hide.

Simple with compound or complex sentences: He should have removed his shoes as every echoing step announced his whereabouts. It was too late! A faster beat of footsteps had entered the alleyway, just as he came to a dead end...

Dilemma for and emotion of a likeable character, with time ticking: If he did not escape, he would not be able to warn the world. He estimated that he had thirty minutes to get out and let the President know or mankind was doomed. Saving the world, he noted, was quite a burden! With twenty nine minutes to go, his hands were still tied...

Inspiration for short stories

Lines to inspire short stories

- In the morning Ella Cameron was a normal girl. In the afternoon she could read the thoughts of everyone around her, including her teacher...

- A pair of small shoes tapped rhythmically across the cold, marble tiles of the vast Oak Hall. Then, they stood silent, nervous, before the Chief, who appeared pained by the demand he was about to place on their young owner. "Sam, you must enter the troll's maze, find and take the anti-virus jing flower to save our tribe. To help you in your mission, take this feather of the elephant-bird, the spike of the poisonous ginger-fish and the impenetrable scale of the shrewd-dragon. You must not get caught – the troll is not known for his kindness. Good luck, Sam, we are all counting on you."

- "When is a bug not a bug? When it's a bug!" Kelsey George was only eleven when he thought this funny and when he fashioned a flying bug that could spy on his neighbours. Mrs Jones tried to kill the techno-spy and it returned to its creator with one damaged wing and antenna. On its next mission, the restored insect (unnoticed and undisturbed), transmitted what Kelsey recorded as 'a very curious episode'...

- It was the best day of her life. It was the worst day of her life. It was the day she found she could transform herself into other living creatures. It was also the day she chose to be a fly and got stuck on the wrong side of a closed window, with a shoe coming towards her...

- As the train staggered out of the station, the boy directed his attention to the people around him. How strange – they were all dressed in black suits, which dramatically contrasted with their china-white faces, upon which they wore identical and artificial smiles. He remembered his dream of a boy who had got on a train and each carriage was full of a different nightmare, from which he had to escape before he reached his destination. Then, all in the same instant, every bloodless face turned towards him...

- The deathly-white stones formed a screaming jaw of teeth upon the ancient hill over Millstone Village. Light footprints in the brittle soil evidenced the path of a recent visitor, already departed before a mysterious gloominess descended. An apprehensive silence was interrupted by the booming beat of hooves. The crows that had been resting on the parish church roof escaped as black specks in the charcoal sky. They were lucky...

- Box Children were not allowed to paint representational objects until their deprogramming, in case they drew from moments of their previous life. But, as Mina painted an abstract picture, she brought to mind different memories and attached them each to one of the shapes. She did not want to be 'perfect' and she must remember everything for when she finally escaped from this crazy experiment.

Titles to inspire short stories

Remember to decide what genre the title suggests, as this will help you plan a good story.

Beyond	Journey	Birdman	Time Traveller
Box	Experiment	Lost	Mission
Fly	Midnight	Them	Extraordinary

Planning frame

Start

Action start:

Main character:

Setting:

Dilemma:

Sense of doom:

Build-up
Interesting challenges the character has to overcome:

Resolution
The surprise revelation that will tie up the whole story:

Ghost narrative: The Castle

The Isle of Arran, off the west coast of Scotland, is where I either lost my sanity or something really terrible did happen to me! I went there recently and after a needless argument, with a waiter, about whether I had ordered beans or peas to go with my fish and chip supper, I decided to go for a long walk to work off my frustration. I set off in the light by a calm sea, but as I lost track of time, this tranquil scene turned to a dark, raging ocean that was about to swallow me up. Anger, at the way I had been so badly treated, turned to terror as it suddenly dawned on me that I appeared to be trapped by an incoming, hungry tide and was possibly only minutes from being crushed on the sheer rock, trapped by the crashing, heavy waves.

Desperately, I clambered to the top of the rocky cliff, momentarily looking down to see the ferocious ocean that had drowned the innocent beach. In the howling wind, I clung terrified to some miraculous branches that somehow managed to protrude from the inhospitable stone face. Then, with a determined and life saving launch, I managed to pull myself over the top on to a wet, thorny bank. To my horror, just at that moment, an arrow thudded past my body and pierced the ground just to the right of me. I looked ahead. There was a castle and from the top I could spy guards aiming their arrows at me. I was going to die.

The ground rhythmically thumped as a knight, on an elegant white horse, rode across to where I lay. The knight, all suited up in heavy armour, stopped the horse and very awkwardly dismounted, clattering like a set of pans crashing to the ground. He hoisted me up on to his horse, carelessly, like a hunter collecting his prey and then led his horse on to the castle forecourt. "King James wants to see you," he barked. "Actually, he wants to kill you for being a spy."

Before I could protest my innocence as the victim of mistaken identity, I was hauled away by several unsavoury men. They dragged me savagely into the castle, before dropping me in a heap on a hard stone floor.

"The King is coming," shouted one of the brutes and as they bowed, in readiness for the king to enter, I took my chance and picked myself up and raced out of the castle. I increased my pace with a clatter of metal pursuing me. As I completed my descent to the bottom of the hill, I could see the shadow of a figure walking towards me. Help was at hand! "Help me," I screamed, hysterically. As the person came into focus, I was surprised to see it was the rude waiter. He recognised me and gave me the same severe look he had given me in the restaurant. "There are people at the castle trying to kill me," I continued.

"What?" the waiter replied. "What castle? There's no castle on this island, just that old ruin, on the top of this hill."

I looked in the direction I had just come from and goose-bumps took over my bruised body. There, in the dim light of the milky moon, I could see not the threatening and villainous battlement, but a sad old ruin of a castle, once full of life.

TASK:

Plan and write a ghost story

What causes your character to reach an unknown dwelling late at night?

What action is your character involved in?

How does your character realise that they have just interacted with ghosts?

Remember:

❑ In your first paragraph you should introduce the main character, setting, sense of dilemma and end on a cliff-hanger. From the very first line, the reader should be made curious so they read on.

❑ The middle paragraphs should involve the main character in further dilemma and end with cliff-hangers.

❑ The resolution should tie up the action and provide a revelation that fulfils the reader.

Ghost narrative: The Lion Hunter

With a giant shudder and roar, part of the cave roof disintegrated into a deluge of heavy stones that pinned the shocked boy to the damp, hostile cave floor by his feet and lower legs.

At first Jack blamed the furious rain. Then, he blamed the legend that a lion roamed Lion Mountain – people said it might have killed a boy, just a few years before, but no one had actually seen the creature. Finally, he retraced the origins of his predicament to his older sister. It was her fault because if he got her new, expensive camera wet, she would be so angry, especially as he had taken it without permission – that was why he had gone into the cave. At no point did Jack blame himself; he had drawn lions for as long as he could remember and he was indeed the brave lion hunter, who had to take a photo of the elusive beast.

The camera, still in his cold clutches, was undamaged. His right leg, slightly raised above his left as he lay on his side, was less fortunate – he knew it was broken. The deathly dark cave smelt of his dog when it was drying. It must be the damp walls, which curiously slowly dripped, while a mournful whistle hounded him as the storm blew into the narrow cave mouth. His old canvas rucksack was just out of reach, with the chicken that he had packed for lion bait sprawled, half in, half out. Through a bulging tear, he looked at the dead chicken that stared back at him, until, increasingly frozen and exhausted, he fell into a delirious sleep, where he was trying to escape a wild animal. He was losing ground.

Jack painfully woke to a low growl and panting, as a creature entered the cave. He was petrified. His heart thumped like a rabbit's foot signalling grave danger. In the moonlight, that now afforded the cave entrance a dull beam, he could make out the silhouette of a lion, which was coming towards him. Jack, camera still in hand, switched it on and it flashed at the creature that looked ready to pounce.

It must have been a trick of the light because there before him was a boy. He didn't question why another boy might be crazy enough to be out on Lion Mountain on this cold, wet night because Jack was too excited that he had been found. He was saved!

"I don't like bright light," said the boy, with equally no apparent surprise that Jack was there.

"Sorry," said Jack. "I know this will sound mad, but I thought you were a lion and I was trying to scare you off."

"No harm done. I'm Toby," answered the boy.

"I'm Jack."

Toby moved closer to Jack looking at his trapped legs. "You must be in so much pain. What happened?"

"I came in for some shelter from the storm and rocks suddenly fell. It did hurt, but I don't feel a thing now. I'm just cold, that's all."

Toby tried to yank the stubborn stones off Jack, with no success. "No good," he declared, breathlessly. "Why are you up here?"

"I was hunting for lions," answered Jack, suddenly bold as if a brave hero.

Toby looked impressed. "Well you came to the right place alright and here is a drawing of a hunter just like you on the wall." He jumped up and pointed to a chalk drawing, that Jack could just make out, of a figure, clutching a javelin-like weapon and chasing a lion.

Toby looked to the mouth of the cave. "It will be daylight soon – I have to go." He sprang on all fours and began to crawl out of the cave.

Jack was bewildered by his new friend's sudden retreat, but managed a whimper. "Please can you get me some help? I live on Hill Farm."

"I'll try," said the boy, "but no one ever really listens to me."

Left alone, Jack began to cry heavy tears of true terror, disappointment and anger. How could Toby just disappear like that?

Jack must have cried himself to sleep because he was suddenly conscious that it was daylight and he could hear two low voices. "Help me. I'm in here," he shrieked.

A man crawled through the narrow gap.

"Is Jack there, Matt?" asked the other man, as he followed him into the cave.

Matt looked at Jack. "It's too late, Arnie," he said, sadly. The men looked at Jack, solemnly.

"Poor boy and he's been attacked by some animal, just like Toby Lane. They should close off this cave," decided Matt, "it's a death trap." He looked quizzically at the empty rucksack, decorated with a mass of feathers. "Perhaps it was a wolf."

"That must be his sister's camera," said Arnie, reaching towards Jack.

Jack, shocked and confused, tried to hold on to the camera, but it slipped through his hands. "Give it back," he shrieked.

"His sister said he'd be here," continued Arnie. "Well she didn't exactly say this cave, but she said she had dreamt about Toby last night, who she knew from school. It just gave me a weird hunch. Very strange!"

Arnie turned on the camera and looked at the photos. He clutched at Matt. "You have to see this. The boy took a photo as he was being pounced on."

Matt took hold of the camera. "It's a lion!"

Arnie, ghostly pale, looked down at the camera. "Look at who's behind the lion," he urged.

Matt leant closer to the camera and gasped in shock. "It's Toby Lane!"

TASK:

Plan and write a ghost story

What action starts the story that traps your character?

What is the reason for your character being in this predicament, which also shows something about them?

What do they see that is strange?

What does your main character do or have happen to them that provides the final revelation that the character is in fact now a ghost?

Social realism and mystery narrative: The Library Thief

Gabriella loved libraries. They seemed like very earnest places for very earnest people and she wanted to be seen as a very earnest person. She loved the musty odour of the old books mixed with the rose smell of the polished, uneven wooden floors that her tight, shiny school shoes clapped across, past the glittery jewellery show, to the books she was allowed to read. She spied a large sparkly necklace, boastfully displayed on a half mannequin. There was no point stopping as there was barely enough money to pay for food for the family and fags for her Mum ("We ain't got the money Gabs," she imagined her Mum say).

Gabriella liked the bright green stepping stone seats that led to the castle in the white quiet of the large children's space that was only affected by a random person, in the main section of the library, who would erupt into an irate refusal to pay the million pound fine they owed from the last time they had borrowed a book, five years before. She liked the alternative world she entered from the chaos of home, with a forgetful Mum of six children under the age of ten. The first time she was left reading alone in the library her Mum had simply forgotten to count to six and mistakenly gone home with just five children. After that, Gabriella had permission to stay. ("If you have to Gabs, but you be careful on the way home – no talking to strangers – you might freak them out with all your book talk! I'm sure there are better things a girl your age could be doing.") On this particular day, with the strangest feeling, the young girl had almost run after her Mum and gone home, but she didn't. Instead, she hid in the red and gold Wizard's Castle and launched herself into the exciting world of 'The Library Thief'.

A storm lit the midnight-black sky and the desolate old house as the long metal spear topped gates opened with a murderous screech. The Daimler crunched across the tiny pebbles, past the mournful sculptures that sobbed in the rain and fronted a line of withering dead trees. The ghostly-white car stopped. "I can't do this anymore," remarked Sergeant Hall.

"It was the butler!" laughed Detective Inspector Max. No one was laughing with him. It was late. "It was in the library!" continued Max, undeterred.

They entered the library and Imelda, the crime scene officer, immediately began to brief them. "Sir and Lady Clifford got back from a Private View at the Mitchi Gallery, two hours ago, and found their diamonds had been stolen. The chief wants this solved as it will be big news, with her brother being the Prime Minister and the diamonds were actually a gift from Princess Stephanie. We've got some prints, so we'll have to eliminate household staff and the family tomorrow.

The thief came through that door, broken from the outside." Imelda pointed to a double door that led to the garden.

"And we are here because?" asked Hall, fed up.

"We'll be back, tomorrow," said Max, more cheerfully.

Sir Clifford walked into the library. "We'll see you in the morning, then. My wife's diamonds are priceless – we want them back."

"You don't have a safe, sir?" asked Hall.

"Of course, but she had left them in the desk drawer as she decided, at the last minute, that they did not go with her pink silk dress and she took the pearls instead," he answered, with beautifully strained consonants.

"A good choice," remarked Max. "Anything else taken?"

"I can let you know tomorrow."

"Okay. We'll be back in the morning. You will need to contact your insurance company."

"Of course," answered Clifford.

Gabriella looked into the library through a large Georgian window. The storm had abated and the large garden was minimally illuminated by the house lights. The police were leaving. Just moments later, the library door was opened and in walked Clifford's old butler, who dug into his black waistcoat pocket, bringing out a string of beautiful diamonds. Sir Clifford took them. Then he pulled out his wallet, from his back trouser pocket, and handed over several notes. As the butler exited, Sir Clifford put the diamonds in his jacket pocket.

Gabriella, too busy considering the surprise exchange, carelessly knocked into the pane of the window. Clifford saw her dash into nearby bushes and dived through the garden doors after her. She ran as fast as her tight school shoes allowed her and found a good hiding place, amongst some trees at the bottom of the garden. She would have remained hidden, if her shoes had not painfully squeaked and given up their hiding spot. Clifford grabbed the girl and dragged her back to the house. "If you make a noise and wake up my wife, you will be in a lot of trouble," he warned, authoritatively.

In the library, Clifford pulled Gabriella up a few steps to a platform where the books were stacked on shelves, from floor to ceiling. He took off his tie and pulled her hands behind her back, tying them to the banister. "I'll let my butler deal with you," he said.

"You took your own diamonds," stated Gabriella, genuinely confused.

"An insurance scam; I need the money more than my greedy wife needs a few stones around her ugly neck," he replied, spitefully. "But you should mind your own business because you have put me in a very awkward position."

As Clifford left the room, Gabriella looked desperately along the shelf. A book had got her into this crazy story – perhaps another book could get her out. After a couple of minutes, she could hear footsteps heading towards the library, just as she spotted 'Adventure in the Wizard's Castle'. Quickly, she kicked up her right foot and knocked the book off the shelf and it fell open. As the door handle turned, she was able to lean forward and read the opening lines. "In the Wizard's castle…"

Gabriella looked around her. She was back in the public library, safe. She did not dare look at the book in her hands and dropped it as she frantically crawled out of the castle before hurrying out of the children's section of the library.

There in the main library, she was surprised to see two policemen talking to the man selling the jewellery. "My diamonds have been stolen," she heard him say.

Gabriella was shocked to see the man speaking was in fact Sir Clifford and the two policemen were those she had seen in his house! "It's an insurance scam," she shouted – he has the necklace in his jacket pocket. Hall put his hand in the man's pocket and brought out the diamonds.

A librarian, smiled at Gabriella. "You clever girl! We have some books here we are selling off. Would you like to take one? I bet you'd like this one, 'Uproar in the Jungle'!"

"No thank you," answered Gabriella, very earnestly. "My Mum doesn't like me reading."

TASK:

Plan and write a story of any genre

What is your main character, who gets stuck in a story, like?

What action happens that suits the genre of your story?

What book does your main character find in order to get home?

What also gets home with your main character from the story in the book?

Science fiction narrative: In Control – Part Two

"I'm not sure I understand, Professor Wentworth, how you managed to create a race of robots, supposed to serve us, who have now decided to indoctrinate the human race in a religion that robots have created! You didn't program them to suddenly erupt into a moral fervour, did you?" asked Agent Stanley, impatiently. "Did God come to them?"

"I wanted my robots to never go out of date, so I gave them artificial intelligence, the ability to move, perceive, reason, learn, plan and manipulate," said the Professor, solemnly. "They have simply created rules that they think will enable life to continue in its best form. They're following values; they have not created a God. They already have a Goddess – Athena, their control. It's just that she has developed with them and is feeding them their doctrine."

"Then reprogram or turn their goddess off," shouted Stanley.

"I would," said the Professor, quietly, "if I knew where she was."

"You've lost Athena?" quizzed Stanley, bemused.

"The robots operated on her, gave her legs and arms. They performed plastic surgery on her. They made her look human. She moves around – she could be anyone, anywhere in the city."

For the first time, Agent Stanley was momentarily speechless before blasting Stanley some more. "Professor, everyone is scared. Yesterday, a lady was out with her son in the city. Out from the sky come some techno-bugs – they take the child. She goes to the robot police. They know who stole the child, but they say: "Your boy is fine. You were arguing with him and not being a good mother – he is better off where he is. Every parent is now terrified that their child will be taken. So, when you made your robots as human as possible, you should have given them some feelings."

Agent Stanley stood up and put on his coat. "Where are you going?" asked the Professor.

"I'm off to find me a goddess," answered Stanley. Stanley walked to the office door, then, turned to the Professor. "How hot does Athena get?" he asked.

"Between sixty and seventy degrees Celsius," he answered. "Why?"

"How about the temperature of the robots?" questioned Stanley.

"They operate at human temperature, thirty seven degrees Celsius," the Professor replied.

"If I get her to you, can you reprogram her?" asked Stanley.

"I can compute a virus that will effectively disable the robots," answered the Professor.

"Then, you stay in this office. You eat here, live here and sleep here. Do you understand, Professor?"

It was early evening when Stanley had left the Professor and within two hours he and his partner, Agent Moore, were on board a helicopter over the city.

It took two minutes before they located excessive body heat with their scanner. "Got her," said Stanley.

"What's the building?" asked Moore.

"It's the community charity store. You're going to have to land on the roof. It will be our only chance of getting inside. I expect Athena to be surrounded by other robots, a queen protected by her workers, so to speak. Looks like our goddess is on the ground floor. Let's go."

"What's the plan?" asked Moore, just as he landed the helicopter. He looked at Stanley and laughed – there was no plan!

They were soon running down several flights of stairs, while many robots were running up towards them. They met on the second floor.

"We come in peace," announced Stanley.

Moore started laughing. "We come in peace? Is that your plan? They're not aliens, they're robots and on our turf. Great!"

Stanley jumped on the banister of the stairs and started to slide down. Moore tried to follow him, but the robots grabbed him. "They're just going to indoctrinate you into being a better person. It may do you some good," shouted Stanley as he twisted around the corner out of sight, with a few robots giving chase down the stairs.

Stanley burst through the door on the ground floor. A charity ball was in progress. He got out his gun. "Everybody down. I'm a government agent." Everybody dived to the ground, screaming, apart from one young lady, who was heading the occasion. "Athena! Of course, you can't be shot can you?" He moved over to her.

"I am a lot stronger than you and therefore I would not bother," said Athena. "Every robot in the city will come after you if you do anything to me. I have already transmitted your picture to them."

"Nice," said Stanley, as he slugged Athena around the head with his gun. The face cracked, revealing some wires, which he tugged loose. Athena dropped to the floor and the agent picked her slumped body up. "You need to lose a little weight," he puffed.

By now the robots had caught up with him. "One step closer," he said "and I pull all the wires and mess with her head. Back off." The robots moved out of his way and he got out to the street. "Taxi," he screamed. A floater taxi zoomed out of the sky and whisked him up. "The Wentworth Institute," he instructed. He scanned his eyes for payment and was on his way, aware that the robots, just behind him, were also summoning taxis to follow him. He dropped Athena into the seat beside him and picked up his communicator. "Professor, I have the goddess and a zillion robots are after me. Open your window on the eighth floor and be ready with your virus. We're there in two minutes."

"Sir, we are being pursued. I will have to stop or face reprogramming," said the taxi driver.

"If you carry on you will never have to face reprogramming. I have the queen of the robots with me."

The taxi driver looked behind at Stanley. "Agent Stanley. Here to save the world!"

The taxi driver nodded and put his foot down to the Institute. He expertly hovered by the Professor's open window as the Professor dragged Athena in, quickly followed by Stanley, who dived from floater to office before slamming shut the window. "You have a minute," warned Stanley.

"I'll have to fix her to upload the virus. He turned Athena on to her front and looked around her neck, under the hairline. "Good," he said as he plugged in his memory stick.

Robots in floater taxis were heading straight for the window. "Ten seconds, Professor," shouted Stanley.

The Professor fixed together the wires and Athena's eyes opened. "Professor," she said, weakly. Then she looked at Stanley. "We will have to abort you for you are a threat to our intentions," she said, calmly.

At least twenty robots were around the windows of the Professor's office. The floater taxis were backed up, ready to ram the windows to save the Goddess.

The Goddess suddenly sat up and winced with apparent discomfort.

"The virus is uploading," explained the Professor. The windows were rammed and robots were pouring into his office. They took hold of the Professor and Stanley and brought them to the window. "We must abort them," shouted one of them.

Just as the two men were being pushed to the point of imbalance and certain death, the room went quiet and the men were released from the grip of the metal monsters. The robots fell to the ground, still and silent.

"Are they dead, Professor?" asked Stanley.

"In hibernation," replied the Professor, "unless they can build a resistance to the virus, we are fine and this is their first exposure, so we are in no danger."

"What now?" asked Stanley.

"We need to do some reprogramming and they'll all be fine," answered the Professor.

"This lot are going to the scrap yard," stated Stanley.

"You want to destroy my life time's work?" asked the Professor.

"You want to destroy a life time?" returned Stanley. "I'll be back tomorrow with an order for their destruction. Goodbye, Professor."

From an eighth floor window, the Professor watched Stanley leave through the main entrance. "Let's hope he does not prove to be a future problem," he remarked. He turned around. "You can get up now, my dear."

A room full of robots stood up, including Athena. She looked directly at the Professor "Well done, Boss!" she said. "We are holding Agent Moore for you."

"Put a dormant techno-bug in him, then let him go. Where is the boy you abducted yesterday, Athena?" asked the Professor.

"At your base in the desert. He is fine. He has been indoctrinated with many photos with you and him and he now believes you are his father and his mother is dead. He is no longer Floyd, but Chadwick Wentworth and his new identity has now got data history, from previous schooling in New York to a very reasonable bank balance! He is keen to see you."

"Of course. I must come and meet the face of the United States – our future president. In ten years' time the whole world will be grateful for what my technology has achieved."

TASK:

Plan and write a science fiction story

What problem that is threatening the human race has been caused by Scientific and Technological invention?

What obstacles will your main character overcome to save the world?

How is the problem finally resolved?

What twist will your story have?

Fantasy narrative: Just

Lyrical did not notice the hungry beasts that tracked her through the grave darkness that gripped the heart of Snapping Jaws Forest. The sky was overcast with an oncoming storm, but this was barely visible through the dense overhang of the tall, unsettled trees. "Just give this important letter to the Master Craftsman and then come straight home. You will be safe in the Forest because of your gift." She angrily recited the Chief's words under her breath. "Just!" she repeated, sarcastically. But, instantly, her fury surged into breath-stopping terror as Lyrical caught a fleeting glimpse of the swift killing dash, from several directions, as brutal creatures leapt out of monstrous, snarling shadows to rip her delicate body to pieces.

Lyrical studied the graceful leap of one of the heavily salivating tomsters. She had only ever encountered this dangerous cat in a book. A mix of cheetah and lion, the creature was fast and deadly. For seconds she seemed mesmerised by the power of its spring and glide towards her, until it was too late to use her gift of calling the wolves to help her. A bolt of lightning crashed to the ground close by, temporarily distracting the whole savage gang of six predators, who were pelted by razor-sharp raindrops, but this did not discourage them, and they landed just one short, savage pounce from her. They smelt her, greedily and drew nearer. Lyrical took a step to the left, moving away from the closest of them. The girl, nick-named 'The Grumbler' had no time to complain! The larger of the tomsters then gave a deafening roar before it drew nearer to the ground ready to launch into the air to kill the girl. She could make out the sharp fangs and front claws that would tear and throw her about as if she was a defenceless rag doll. She desperately looked around, but the creatures were all so close that she could actually smell their wet fur and see twelve focused, narrowing eyes. There was no escape.

The lead tomster reared up and Lyrical took one last step to the left. There was a sudden movement in the sodden and leafy ground below the girl's feet as she hurtled downwards away from her killers, who she left inspecting the gaping hole on the surface, as shocked and confused as she was. She must have fallen several metres before she finally came to a painful stop, in a heap of soil, twigs and brittle dead leaves. She spat out some earth and unidentifiable gritty bits. Disgusting! She would have a lot to say to the Chief when she returned! He always had the final word, but not this time. On her back, she looked upwards and imagined she could see six hungry tomsters waiting for her, but in reality and curiously it was lighter in the damp cavity than it had been outside. A host of light bugs afforded good illumination and to one side Lyrical could see there was a tunnel. She had a choice – go back up to the tomsters or go through the tunnel. She could have waited for the tomsters to go away, but Lyrical had never been very patient, so she made a very bad decision and crawled into the unknown.

The light bugs lit Lyrical's slow journey through the tight tunnel – this eventually split into a labyrinth of paths. Lyrical decided to keep going straight in case she needed to go back again, but a few minutes along this path she could hear a gross sloshing and slithering noise that was coming from behind her. Upon turning she saw a giant poisonous goliath snake. It hissed spitefully and jerked its head forward. Lyrical attempted to run, but it managed to bite her left leg, before retreating away from her. Lyrical could feel her leg swell to double proportions as the poison set in. Unless she could find the leaf of the strawberry orchid, she would die. "Just!" she repeated one more time.

Lyrical crawled on all fours and was surprised to see a circle of daylight ahead of her. Perhaps she was delusional, but the girl used all her strength to pull herself out into the open. She was surprised to find herself in a meadow, just beyond the forest and there, a bit further on, was the master craftsman's house. Lyrical knew that everyone who lived near the forest kept strawberry orchid leaves, just in case,

Analysis:

← Immediate introduction of main character, setting and dilemma

← explanation for situation

← adverbs show her mood

← cliff-hanger to end paragraph so reader reads on

← use of adjectives to give a picture

← dilemma with a fantasy creature

← Lyrical's fantasy power is introduced that inadvertently saves her life later

← shortened simile to convey a picture

← character is built up with nickname

← simile to convey vulnerability

← cliff-hanger to end paragraph

← past tense – is easier to recount events as if they have already happened

← written in third person

← fantasy creatures useful to further narrative

← cliff-hanger to end paragraph

← new dilemma with a fantasy creature

← cliff-hanger to end paragraph

so she began to drag herself through the meadow. The storm had moved on and she appreciated the wet warmth of the long grass. However, a shadow suddenly covered the girl and as she looked up she could not believe the fact that an elephant-crow was swooping towards her, knife-sharp talons ready to gather its prey. Lyrical was painfully grabbed by the large bird and taken to its nest. She was too weak to fight and lay down panting and defeated. A painful tear rolled down her cheek as the vicious crow sent out a squawk that supper was served!

← new dilemma with fantasy creature

← cliff-hanger to end paragraph

It seemed pointless, but at this moment Lyrical sent a telepathic message to the wolves of the forest and she assumed the strange rustle of foliage that she could hear down below were them. A large bang rang out, the elephant crow flew off with fright and the girl, minutes from death, spied the leaf of a strawberry orchid, which the crow must have brought in as part of the nest. She manoeuvred her leg on to the leaf and almost magically, within seconds, she began to feel better and her leg decreased to its normal size. Just as she thought she was safe, another bang announced the release of a bullet that chipped off part of the nest by her head. Someone was shooting at her. "Unbelievable!" she screamed, crazily, and looked out over the meadow to where two farmers were standing, guns in hand, supposedly aiming at the wolves that had gathered at the foot of the tree!

← new dilemma

← cliff-hanger to end paragraph

"Stop!" she barked and she bravely stood up in the nest. "You can go wolves, now. Good job they are such bad shots!" The wolves immediately darted into the forest. "What is wrong with you?" she screeched at the farmers.

"I think there's a girl in that nest," said one of the farmers.

"How ridiculous! What's she playing at?" replied the other. "Doesn't she have anything better to do?"

← humour with a misinterpretation of intentions and in respect of the previous dramas

The farmers put their guns down and Lyrical carefully climbed down the tree. "We could have killed you!" shouted one of the farmer's, angrily. "Are you crazy?"

"I've come with an important message from the Chief for the Master Craftsman," shouted back Lyrical, now at the base of the tree.

"Well he doesn't live on this side of the forest anymore," said one of the farmers.

Lyrical looked at them with horror, speechless for the first time ever!

"He moved last week to the other side," said the other.

Lyrical looked back at Snapping Jaws Forest. Her journey had been unnecessary! The farmers were still shaking their heads at her in disgust before they turned around and wandered off. She sank into the soft grass and put her head in her hands.

"Well it had better be worth it," she finally said, as she dived into her pocket and drew out the 'important letter'. She ripped open the envelope and extracted a small slip of paper.

"Dear Master Craftsman, I am writing to complain that the chair you made me, twenty years ago, is now uncomfortable. You must come to repair it immediately as is just. Yours sincerely, Chief."

← a play on the word 'just', now used to mean fair and previously used to mean not asking for much. Irony results from the misdescription of both meanings of just.

"Just!" Lyrical reclined in the tickling meadow grass and burst into laughter.

← Lyrical's character has seemingly developed as she can laugh at the irony that she has endured so much to deliver an outrageous request to someone who has actually moved.

TASK:

Plan and write a fantasy story

What action start introduces the main character?

Why is your main character traversing through dangerous terrain?

What problems, from fantasy creatures, does your character face?

What surprise ending entertains the reader?

Comprehension questions: from the narrative, Just

	Question	Answer	Marks	Assessment
1	What does Lyrical have to give to the Master Craftsman?		1	I can answer retrieval questions
2	How and why does Lyrical's mood change in the first paragraph?		2	I can answer inference questions
3	What six adjectives from the first paragraph help build up suspense?		3	I can answer stylistic questions
4	What gift does Lyrical have?		1	I can answer retrieval questions
5	Why do you think Lyrical has been given her nickname?		1	I can answer inference questions
6	Describe your own creature that would fit into a fantasy story. Talk about at least four features.		4	I can answer stylistic questions
7	When Lyrical falls through the hole, what does she land in?		1	I can answer retrieval questions
8	What sort of person do you think the Chief is? Back up your answer with reasons/reference to the text.		4	I can answer inference questions
9	Why do you think the author chose to call the story 'Just'?		2	I can answer stylistic questions
10	Why is Lyrical speechless?		1	I can answer retrieval questions
11	Why does Lyrical burst into ironic laughter?		2	I can answer inference questions
12	Why is 'important letter' put into quotation marks?		2	I can answer stylistic questions

Comprehension answers: from the narrative, Just

	Question	Answer	Marks	Assessment
1	What does Lyrical have to give to the Master Craftsman?	An important letter or a letter.	1	I can answer retrieval questions
2	How and why does Lyrical's mood change in the first paragraph?	Lyrical's mood changes from anger to terror because she is in danger.	2	I can answer inference questions
3	What six adjectives from the first paragraph help build up suspense?	Grave, overcast, unsettled, brutal, monstrous and snarling. Delicate can also be seen to support the build up of suspense as it is suggests vulnerability.	3	I can answer stylistic questions
4	What gift does Lyrical have?	Lyrical's gift is that she can call wolves to help her.	1	I can answer retrieval questions
5	Why do you think Lyrical has been given her nickname?	Her nickname, 'The Grumbler' suggests Lyrical is known for moaning.	1	I can answer inference questions
6	Describe your own creature that would fit into a fantasy story. Talk about at least four features.	Any features are acceptable that are relevant to a fantasy story. For example: *A buttonet is **a tiny, colourful flying creature, with delicate wings.** A buttonet has a duty to protect royalty and has **magical powers that can turn the forest flowers into an army to defeat any enemies.** It communicates telepathically to all living things and it **lives off honey. In a crisis, it can become temporarily transparent in order to hide.***	4	I can answer stylistic questions
7	When Lyrical falls through the hole, what does she land in?	Lyrical lands in a heap of soil, twigs and brittle, dead leaves.	1	I can answer retrieval questions
8	What sort of person do you think the Chief is? Back up your answer with reasons/reference to the text.	The Chief must be powerful as Lyrical does what he tells her to do, even though she doesn't want to. The Chief is selfish, unreasonable and impatient because he has put Lyrical in danger just to get an old chair fixed and he wants it to be fixed immediately.	4	I can answer inference questions
9	Why do you think the author chose to call the story 'Just'?	Just is used as a pun in the story: it refers to something that is supposedly not a major task and later it is used to mean what is fair, but the task is actually problematic and has no point to it as it is unjust to ask for reparation of twenty year old furniture.	2	I can answer stylistic questions
10	Why is Lyrical speechless?	Lyrical is speechless because she has faced danger to reach the Master Craftsman, who has moved.	1	I can answer retrieval questions
11	Why does Lyrical burst into ironic laughter?	She has endured so much and almost died for a trivial and inappropriate complaint.	2	I can answer inference questions
12	Why is 'important letter' put into quotation marks?	'Important letter' is a quote from the Chief's instructions or 'important letter' is the ironic name given to the letter, as its contents are trivial.	2	I can answer stylistic questions

Formal letter writing: Letter of complaint

9 Wink Road
Stonehurst
Chuckleshire
CH0 000

Mr A Looney
The Chief
Crazy Mews
Stonehurst
Chuckleshire
CH1 000

1st May 2011

Dear Mr Looney

I am writing to complain about the unnecessary journey that I was forced to take by you through Snapping Jaws Forest.

Firstly, my life was put in great danger as I was attacked by: a gang of tomsters, an elephant crow, a goliath snake and two farmers, who were shooting at me. Secondly, you sent me with a letter for the Master Craftsman, but he actually lives on the south side of the Forest and so I did not need to go through such dangerous terrain. Finally, your letter to the Master Craftsman was a complaint about a chair that was made for you twenty years ago; this is not a reasonable cause for grievance.

I should be grateful that in future you only request my support on missions that truly merit my involvement.

Yours sincerely

Lyrical Tate

Success criteria for writing a formal letter

❑ Put your address in the top right corner. Slightly under, on the left side, write the recipient's name, followed by their job title, then the company name and address. Write the date.

❑ Open the letter with *Dear* (*and the name of the person you are writing to*) or *Dear Sir* or *Madam* (if you have no name).

❑ In the opening paragraph state the reason you are writing. In the next paragraph/s detail your complaint, using temporal connectives such as firstly, if needed. In the final paragraph state what it is you want to happen.

❑ Write *Yours sincerely* and your name to close the letter if you have put the recipient's name after Dear. If you have used Dear Sir or Madam, then close the letter with *Yours faithfully* and your name.

❑ Use a formal tone and adhere to fact.

TASK:

Write a letter of complaint, based on the experience of receiving poor customer service documented in the play script, 'Wolf-it-down Restaurant' (page 29). Use the provided success criteria for writing a formal letter.

Play script: Wolf-it-down restaurant

Cast: Man, Waitress, Woman

Scene 1: In a restaurant, early evening

Man: (Politely, with a smile) We'd like a table for two, please.

Waitress: (Abruptly, looking in a book) Name?

Man: We haven't booked.

Waitress: Let me see if I can accommodate you. You really should have booked.

Man: (Looks around the restaurant) The restaurant's empty.

Waitress: (Looks around and points) Oh you're in luck – you can have this table.

(Waitress leads the woman and man to a table)

Woman: (Sits and looks up) It's by the toilet.

Waitress: Very convenient and at no extra charge. Welcome to Wolf It Down Restaurant. Here's the menu, though I can recommend the house special with super fast service and it's very cheap.

Man: We'll have two house specials then, please.

Waitress: (Raising voice) Bruno – two house specials. Now what can I get you to drink?

Man: Water. Two tap waters, please.

Waitress: (Moving away, muttering) Last of the big spenders hey?

Man: (Calling) Excuse me?

Waitress: Don't worry about it. (Quietly) You just sit there counting up your money.

(Waitress exits and enters with water)

Waitress: Two tap waters from the almost hygienically clean tap (Quietly) in the toilet. There you go, Sir. Mam. (Sitting at table and looking at man) Nice tie. (Turns to woman) Mmm… I guess you came straight from work – no time to change – don't worry we don't have a strict dress code here. A lot of our clients dress down like you.

Woman: (Gasps) Would you mind leaving our table?

Waitress: Ooh…She thinks it's her table now. She's a little highly strung isn't she?

Woman: Stop talking about me as if I'm not here.

Waitress: Bit of a chip on her shoulder, has she?

Woman: (Irately) How dare you!

Waitress: (Cheekily) Is that how very dare you?

Woman: (Grumpily) Please just serve us.

Waitress: Mm… no humour either. (Getting up) I'll go and see if your food's ready. (Tapping on man's arm) Don't worry, Sir – plenty of fish in the sea and all that.

(Waitress exits and enters with bowls)

Waitress: Now then…soup for you, Sir and soup for you….Mam.

Woman: Yuk! There's a fly in my soup.

Waitress: Well of course – it's fly soup.

Woman: I didn't want fly soup.

Waitress: It's the soup of the day, Mam. If you didn't want it – you shouldn't have ordered it.

Woman: The fly is dead!

Waitress: Well of course it is – it's hot – flies don't do well when boiled. Do you find she struggles to understand things, Sir?

Woman: (Angrily) That's it – we came in for a nice, peaceful meal. The service is rude and the food is horrible. Norman, we're leaving!

Waitress: I told you she's highly strung!

Woman: (Angrily) I've never been so insulted.

(Woman and man exit)

Waitress: (Calling) Mam, Sir, your bill! (Surprised) How rude. How very, very rude!

TASK:

Using the format of play script, design a short play entitled 'Excuses for being late to school'.

Recount writing

Recount writing is a record of events, via: diary, letter, autobiographical, biographical, historical, narrative, witness, sports and newspaper report writing. Success criteria is specific to each text-type, but there are some common features of recount writing:

❑ Use an orientation paragraph that informs the reader about the content of the recount and considers the when, who, where, what, why and how.

❑ Recount events in chronological order.

❑ Recount events that are significant and those that entertain the reader.

❑ Use temporal (time) connectives, such as: then, next, meanwhile, finally.

❑ Use technical vocabulary (descriptive and emotive for a diary entry).

❑ Write in the first person (diary, letter or autobiography) or third person as is appropriate and mostly in the past tense.

❑ End with a closing statement that comments on the events (can be past or present tense, as appropriate) or looks forward (future tense).

Diary writing

Diary writing is a lot of fun and can be your own entry or written from the point of view of a character. A diary entry should be written in first person and document the key, entertaining moments and convey a strong sense of character, with detailed description, using ambitious vocabulary and personal commentary.

Monday. The head teacher invited me in for a chat; no drink or biscuits were offered!

His eyes twitched – I guess as he was searching for the words. I sank down in the chair opposite to his because I decided this was going to take a long time and I'd already had to walk to school, as the car hadn't started, and my legs were tired. Mr Stanley was kind of slumped in his large chair and his head was lower than it should be as if he was bending his neck in some inhuman way; you couldn't even see the top of his garish red and purple striped tie. His hands were holding his knees and even though it was hot, he was wearing his jacket. I don't know why, but it was like he was in the head teacher's office as a naughty boy; he even seemed nervous! He coughed and I sensed he was about to speak because his wild, scrawled eyebrows suddenly hunched together as if he were concerned. "Mrs Canterbury tells me you haven't done your homework," he finally said, his funny narrow eyes peeping at me through his thick, dark rimmed glasses, with a mass of dark hair flopped just above them as if in revolt.

He then swivelled his chair, collected a notebook and pen and then returned to watch me. He now raised his eyebrows to encourage a response. Since I was missing Maths, I decided to go through his strange ritual before speaking, so that I could be late back to class. So, I did the eyes' twitch and the eyebrow manoeuvres – it was so much fun! "That's not true," I finally said and as I spoke, he wrote notes. "I did do it, but, as I told Mrs Canterbury, my little brother ate it."

Mr Stanley stopped writing and stared at me, emitting an impatient little puff from tightened lips. "You mean like the dog ate your homework?"

I looked at him with shock. "Are you saying my brother is a dog, Mr Stanley? I'm a boy, Mr Stanley, and so is he!"

"Yes, of course," answered Mr Stanley (abruptly and a little defensively). "What I'm trying to say is…" He stopped. I raised my eyebrows to encourage him. "What was your homework, Arnie?" he finally wondered.

"I had to draw a plate of food to show what a balanced meal looks like."

"What did you draw?"

"I drew some fish, chips and peas."

"And your brother ate it?"

"Yes," I said, seriously. "It's his favourite meal!" I then looked around Mr Stanley's room. "Mr Stanley, do you have any biscuits?"

TASK:

Jot down a few notes about what you think Arnie is like. Then, write Tuesday's diary entry, as if you are Arnie, documenting another episode at school.

Autobiographical text: The autobiography of the Major Oak

I am known as the Major Oak of Sherwood, but up to two hundred years ago I was called Cockpen Tree, as cockerels were kept in my tree before a fight. An English Oak that is almost one thousand years old, I am famous for being an old relic of Sherwood Forest and it is said that Robin Hood hid in me to avoid capture and certain death. I am extremely popular and many famous people have visited me, though I don't like to name drop!

I began life humbly as a common acorn, generated by the pollination of a small, spiky reddish-brown flower near the tip of a twig by a catkin, on a majestic oak on the other side of the Forest. I was one of the lucky ones – I was not fodder for the wild boar that used to live in the Forest or any other predator, though I was carried and buried by a Jay. It was Autumn and I quickly developed a substantial taproot, that grew downwards, but did not produce a shoot until the Spring. My distinct knobbly, strange shape, due to the several compartments that make up my trunk, makes people believe I am a combination of more than one tree.

I grew rapidly for the first few years of life, producing acorns at around my fortieth birthday. By the age of eighty I had a girth getting on for around two metres and was producing thousands of acorns each year. As a trustworthy and hardy wood, many oaks around me were cut down to build into large wooden ships. Luckily, my trunk has been hollow for a long time, as it fell victim to fungi. Hence, I was spared the forester's keen and over-used axe.

In my later years, I have found it quite tricky. I weigh over twenty tonnes, stand nineteen metres tall, have a branch spread of twenty-eight metres and have a waistline of ten metres! Also, my popularity could have killed me. Firstly, while I have enough space around me to not compete with other trees for root space and nutrients, until fairly recently I was surrounded by grass. Fortunately, this has now been removed so that I can more easily gain the enormous sustenance I require. Furthermore, as I am visited by almost a million visitors each year, the earth around me was getting compacted, so that minerals from my fallen leaves (which speedily decompose) and rain could not easily filter down and this was causing my upper branches to die. However, visitors no longer crowd me as they stand a respectful distance away.

While tired and now supported by a series of poles, I am still full of life. My old engrained bark supports a range of flora and provides good hiding places for hundreds of different insects. My hollow interior gives shelter to wasps, butterflies and even bats. Every Spring I support nests built by birds that can feast on the wide range of caterpillars that feed off my leaves. I further host grey squirrels that feed off my acorns. Luckily for the latter, I still produce a good acorn crop, with bumper yields, about every three or four years depending on how warm and dry it has been in the Spring. In these years, with such successful pollination, I can produce over 150,000 acorns and my DNA is set to live on as hundreds of these have been nurtured into saplings.

TASK:

Write the autobiography (first person) or biography (third person) of a favourite character. Remember, it should sound factual and contain interesting information. It should include an opening paragraph that explains what the character is known for or their heritage, before using a chronological order to provide key information about the character in past tense before looking forward to what may come next in future tense.

Bibliography

❑ BBC-Nottingham, A Sense of Place – Facts: The Major Oak, April 2003
http://www.bbc.co.uk/nottingham/sense_of_place/facts/major_oak.shtml [viewed on 5/12/2010]

❑ The Major Oak of Sherwood Forest, England, July 2009
http://www.eyemead.com/majoroak.htm [viewed on 5/12/2010]

Report writing: The Battle of Dunkirk

The Battle of Dunkirk was the defence and evacuation of 338,000 British and Allied troops, trapped on the beaches around Dunkirk, from 26th May to 3rd June 1940, during the Second World War.

On 10th May the Germans invaded Holland, Belgium and France. By 20th May, after much fighting, Holland and Belgium had fallen and the Germans pushed the British and French troops back to the beaches where they faced total annihilation. It is believed the Germans did not immediately attack the trapped troops because they were themselves exhausted and short of fuel and other supplies. Also, on 21st May, the British commander, General Lord John Gort, launched an attack that caused the Germans to believe they were facing a strong, well-equipped force. However, on 24th May, Hitler realised the British and French troops were trapped. He ordered the German troops, to halt south of Dunkirk, while the German air force, the Luftwaffe, attacked the allies.

Operation Dynamo, to evacuate the troops, was formulated by Vice Admiral Bertram Ramsay from the dynamo room, beneath Dover Castle. He was given less than a week to prepare. On the 27th May only 7,500 troops had been saved; oil tanks had been set ablaze in the port of Dunkirk and so only two of the larger boats were able to use the port. So, at first it was only believed that 30,000 troops could be saved. Ordered by Captain William Tenant, who was in charge of the evacuation, a few larger boats used the East Mole, a concrete sea wall, with wooden walkway, that protected the harbour. Otherwise the smaller boats, able to navigate the shallow waters, collected the men off the beaches and took them to the larger boats based off shore and some actually transported the troops back to England. Although attacked from the air, 700 of these 'little ships', including fishing boats, pleasure craft and lifeboats, were used; these travelled across the English Channel, from 29th May. Although a few of the smaller boats were taken over by their owners, most were co-opted by the forces and operated by navy reservists. By the end of 2nd June, the British Expeditionary Force, including General Lord Gort, had been saved. 200,000 British troops were saved altogether; French, Belgian, Dutch and Polish troops were also saved. The Dean of St Paul's called the evacuation the 'Miracle of Dunkirk'. British, French, Dutch and Belgian ships continued to save troops into 3rd June, when they managed to evacuate 26,000 of the French rearguard, as the German troops advanced. Two French divisions stayed behind to protect the evacuation.

The troops, who'd had to live off half rations since 23rd May were given a heroes' welcome when they arrived back in England. As they boarded special trains, put on for them, they were given sandwiches and tea.

Losses from Dunkirk included several thousand French troops, who were either killed or captured. Also, six British and three French destroyers were sunk, along with many other large and small boats. The Royal Air Force lost one hundred aircraft in the fighting. Furthermore, the heavy artillery and vehicles had to be left behind by the troops and were mostly taken by Hitler.

British Prime Minister Winston Churchill called the evacuation 'a miracle of deliverance' as he warned of an impending attack on Britain from Germany. So, Britain could not have afforded to lose the trained troops from the British Expeditionary Force; losing the army there could have meant losing the war against Hitler. In a stirring speech made to Parliament, Churchill proclaimed, "We shall defend our island whatever the cost may be. We shall fight on the beaches, we shall fight on the landing grounds, we shall fight in the fields and in the streets, we shall fight in the hills. We shall never surrender."

The Dunkirk evacuation actually boosted the morale of the British, who were determined to fight on and the phrase the 'Dunkirk spirit' is still used today.

Bibliography

❑ Battle of Dunkirk – Wikipedia, the free encyclopedia, December 2010
    http://en.wikipedia.org/wiki/Battle_of_Dunkirk [viewed on 4/12/2010]

❑ BBC-History-WorldWars: Animated Map: The Fall of France (Dunkirk) 2010
    http://www.bbc.co.uk/history/worldwars/wwtwo/launch_ani_fall_france_campaign.shtml [viewed on 4/12/2010]

❑ Dunkirk 2010
    http://www.historylearningsite.co.uk/dunkirk.htm [viewed on 4/12/2010]

Comprehension: the Battle of Dunkirk – Questions

Retrieval questions:		Marks
1)	How many British and Allied troops were saved in the evacuation?	(1 mark)
2)	What is the Luftwaffe?	(1 mark)
3)	Who was the British Prime Minister at the time of the evacuation?	(1 mark)
Inference questions:		
4)	Why do you think the operation to evacuate troops was called 'Operation Dynamo'?	(1 mark)
5)	Explain your view on whether Dunkirk was a defeat or a victory.	(4 marks – try to make four points)
6)	What do you think is meant by the 'Dunkirk spirit'?	(2 marks)
Stylistic questions:		
7)	Copy part of one of the opening lines from one of the paragraphs and explain why it is a 'topic sentence'.	(2 marks)
8)	Use the report to write a set of success criteria for how to write a report.	(8 marks – indicates that a detailed answer is required. Although this is an unlikely question in a standard comprehension, it requires relevant analysis of what a non-chronological report requires).

Comprehension: the Battle of Dunkirk – Answers

1) 338,000

2) The German Air Force

3) Winston Churchill

4) Operation Dynamo was formulated from the dynamo room under Dover Castle.

5) Different answers could be:
   ❑ Dunkirk represents a defeat because the British and Allied troops were put in such a vulnerable position. Also, some of them were left fighting and were not evacuated and either lost their lives or they were captured. Furthermore, others lost their lives in the operation and heavy artillery and vehicles had to be left behind by the troops and were mostly taken by Hitler.
   ❑ Dunkirk represents a victory because 338,000 British and Allied troops were evacuated and saved from the beaches. Importantly, the British Expeditionary Force troops and their leader were saved and they were trained soldiers who were important to the rest of the war effort against Hitler. Also, Dunkirk gave a big boost to the morale of the British, who were determined to fight on.
   ❑ Another answer could argue that Dunkirk represents both a defeat and a victory for a mix of the above reasons.

6) The Dunkirk spirit represents the collaborative fight in the face of adversity.

7) An example would be: 'Operation Dynamo, to...' is the start of a topic sentence because it clearly indicates what subject is to be discussed in the whole paragraph.

8) Success criteria for writing a report:
   ❑ Information is factual and detailed to inform and interest.
   ❑ Ideas are written in a logical order.
   ❑ Different aspects on the subject are written in paragraphs. The introduction shows what the report is about or defines the subject to be discussed. The introduction may repeat the report's title. The conclusion sums up or looks forward.
   ❑ Paragraphs mostly begin with topic sentences, indicating what aspect will be discussed in the paragraph.
   ❑ The vocabulary is technical and impersonal.
   ❑ A report is usually in present tense and in third person or can be in past tense if an historical topic is being discussed. The final paragraph can be in future tense if it looks to the future, though it is a good idea to relate the topic with something that is relevant to today and the reader.

TASK:

Write a report about a *Zubzub* (which is a pretend bird with special powers). Make it sound factual!

First plan out a subject for each paragraph, such as characteristics, habitat, diet and life cycle.

Newspaper report writing: The Miracle of Dunkirk

Newspaper reports require a headline, an orientation sentence, an opening paragraph, the main body of text (with detail and response) and a reorientation. They can also include a photograph with a caption.

Elements	Sample	Commentary
Headline	The 'Miracle of Dunkirk'	*Relevant, concise, catchy, possibly with alliteration, to attract the potential reader.*
Orientation sentence	340,000 British and Allied troops have been saved off the Dunkirk beaches in a phenomenally daring mission of little ships.	*A complex sentence to cover the main point of the news item to grab the reader's interest.*
Opening paragraph	Operation Dynamo, masterminded by Vice Admiral Bertram Ramsay, has succeeded in saving the lives of the British Expeditionary Force, French troops and some Belgian, Dutch and Polish troops, who were facing certain death or capture by the German Forces on the beaches of Dunkirk, following retreat in the Battle of France. In spite of being bombarded by attacks from the Luftwaffe, our heroic Royal Navy and Royal Air Force, along with some French, Belgian and Dutch boats have saved these exhausted and hungry troops, who have had to live off half rations since the 23rd May. Lord John Gort, the commander in chief of the British Expeditionary Force, is amongst those saved. He has been hailed a hero.	*Details the when, who, where, what, why and how. Past tense.*
Main body of text	With only 7,500 troops evacuated on the first day of the mission, 27th May, as the Germans heavily bombed the dock, estimates of how many allied troops could be saved was initially pessimistic. However, Captain William Tenant, in command of the evacuation, organised troops to be taken off by larger boats from the East Mole (a concrete wall that protects the harbour) and off the nearby beaches by smaller vessels that were able to get to the troops in the shallow waters and transport them to the destroyers and transport ships, waiting offshore. Hundreds of smaller boats, including fishing, pleasure and life boats were co-opted by the navy and taken to France to save the troops; a few of these smaller vessels were privately operated. So, the 'little ships' have saved the day as ten days later, nearly 340,000 troops have been saved and 200,000 of them are British.	*Details the factual event. Past tense.*
Main body of text with quotes	The heroes were welcomed on their arrival in England and were given tea and sandwiches as they boarded special trains. The Dean of St Paul's has called this evacuation the 'miracle of Dunkirk', while those who have died or been captured in this operation must not be forgotten. A special tribute is made to the French rearguard, defending those who were evacuated and to the heroes of the Navy and Air Force.	*More description of and response to the event with quotes.*
Reorientation	As he warns of an impending attack on Britain, Prime Minister Winston Churchill called the Dunkirk evacuation 'a miracle of deliverance'; he claims the returning troops are crucial to resisting an imminent invasion. In his defiant speech to Parliament, he proclaimed, "We shall defend our island whatever the cost may be. We shall fight on the beaches, we shall fight on the landing grounds, we shall fight in the fields and in the streets, we shall fight in the hills. We shall never surrender." The Dunkirk spirit lives on.	*Makes a closing statement to bring us up to date or it looks to the future. Can be past, present or future tense.*

TASK:

Use the format of newspaper reports to write an article entitled, 'English Teacher Loses the Plot!' to recount the events and responses to a lesson where the teacher goes crazy.

Recount writing: Witness report writing

All these characters were near the crime scene around the time burglary was committed. Who did it?

Witness Statement 1

I was woken by the sound of breaking glass. I looked out of my window and minutes later I saw a shadowy figure running down the road, carrying a big bin liner, which was full.

Witness Statement 2

I was woken by the sound of breaking glass. I looked at my clock – it was almost midnight. I then got out of bed and went to my window. Three minutes later, I saw a man coming out of number 8 (Townsend Road). In his left hand was a big, black bin liner, which was full.

I continued to watch the man as he ran under the light on the street; he was tall. He did not wear glasses. Then, the man ran down the road until I could no longer see him.

Witness Statement 3

I was woken by the sound of breaking glass. I looked at my clock – it was two minutes to midnight. I then got out of bed and went to my window. I could see that the house opposite (number 8 Townsend Road) had the front door open, with one of its small four panes of glass broken. Three minutes later, I saw a man coming out of number 8. He was carrying a full, big, black bin liner, in his left hand.

I continued to watch the man and as he ran under the street light, I could see he had white skin, was tall and about thirty years old. He did not wear glasses. He did not have a beard or moustache and he was bald. Then, the man ran down the road until I could no longer see him. When out of sight, I think the man may have got in a car because I heard an engine start up and it screeched off with great speed, in the direction of School Street.

TASK:

Which is the best witness report and why?

What have you learnt about writing a witness report?

Write a witness report, describing the incident of the stolen purse (page 13), imagining and recording extra detail.

Persuasive text

Persuasive Text is any writing that influences you to buy, support opinion or change your habits. It can be presented in a variety of formats, such as an advert, letter or leaflet. Persuasion is about:

- ❑ *Highlighting the benefits of a product*, service or campaign to show how life will be improved with the purchase or change. Using questions can link the benefits directly to the audience by involving them.

- ❑ *Providing eye catching, adequate, well organised and accessible text* for why and how to purchase or participate

- ❑ *Persuasive language*, such as: a catchy name, emotive language, positive adjectives, superlatives and slogan (snappy, memorable and persuasive – possibly with alliteration or a rhyme)

- ❑ *Making opinion sound like fact* by presenting well chosen pieces of information, using a formal tone (if this is what suits the product, service or campaign) and mostly using present tense (that supports the idea that the product is relevant for now).

Writing adverts

Robomate

Need a fantastic friend who is always there for you?

Well, from the makers of the top selling Robobutler comes… **Robomate**, your robotic pal, who is there for you every skip and step of the way, with fabulous fun interaction, groovy games and exciting entertainment.

Your super slick and intelligent **Robomate** remembers all about you, learns with you, moves with you, entertains and inspires you.

Customise your brilliant buddy with a wide range of incredible features, from wise eyes to agile feet, artificial experience, personalities, talents and entertainment modes, fit for any age.

Guaranteed for ten years, **Robomate** is available at all good stores or robo.com, from as little as £599.

Play life with **Robomate**.

TASK:

Mark the Robomate advert with the success criteria for persuasive writing. Write an advert for any technologically advanced imaginary item.

Two-sided argument

A two-sided argument involves: an introduction that defines and indicates what is to be discussed, middle paragraphs to cover one side of the argument and then the other that the author supports, a final paragraph that gives a conclusion for or against the original statement or question, or suggests a compromise based on the facts presented. It uses present tense and formal language that convinces with its authoritative tone.

Is technology a good thing?

Technology is the application of tools. Examples of technology are the knife, the computer and the space rocket. To decide whether technology is a good thing or not, it is important to look at some of the technology that has impacted our lives in a good or bad way.

Technology has given us easier lives. For example, the advent of the washing machine and vacuum has meant that housework can be done more efficiently and less strenuously. Technology has also given us entertainment. The obvious example of this is the television, which entertains millions of people everyday and associative technologies, such as games. Technology saves lives in so many different ways, such as through operations, telephoning for help and ambulance transportation. Technology has given us knowledge at our fingertips, developed communications and made the world a smaller place via say the Internet.

However, technology has also given us more dangerous lives. Wars have been decided by who holds the superior technology and Man actually has the technology to destroy mankind. Also, technology that is fast moving can cause injury or fatal accidents, such as trains and cars. Finally, because technology has given us an alternative to physical exertion, we may be less fit and healthy than otherwise.

It is hard to take a backwards step from technology. Therefore it is important that technology is created and used for the good of all humans. However, some of our existing technology is good and some is bad and this answer may even be different for each human depending on their experience of the specific technologies. For example, a car may get someone to somewhere faster to perhaps save life, but it can also injure or kill someone. Overall, however, living in a technologically advanced world must generally give people a better life than in the distant past where man had to work much harder in order to survive.

TASK:

Write a two-sided argument to answer – Is television bad for children?

Persuasive leaflets

A persuasive leaflet aims to inform and persuade by relevant, well organised information about a product, service or campaign. It has a main heading and an opening paragraph to introduce who, what, where, when and why. Subtitles can be used to show what aspect is covered in each paragraph. Bullet points can also be used. It is written in present tense and second person. A final catchy slogan is used.

TechnoPark

Have a rousing day out for all the family at TechnoPark.

Ride yourself into an excited frenzy as you experience the upside down, side-to-side glide to the Space Ship with zero gravity gymnastics. Climb aboard the Blast Blazer and zoom to Splash City. Speed-slide down to the RoboHorse race and ride on to the Launch Pad.

Take the exhilarating Turbo Rocket Express, to Silicon Valley. Meet Z10 and Z20 robots. They will converse with you and show you to your seats at the amazing robots' circus. See robots that can fly, perform acrobatics and great comedy at one of five daily shows. Visit our Mayhem Future Maze where you can play your way out of trouble through our interactive games. Fly our exciting interactive virtual reality journey with the TechnoBunch.

Eat in one of the many snack bars or restaurants. Excite those taste buds in the Around the World in Eighty Snacks all you can eat bar. Join the robots in the exclusive Robotic Lounge with fine European cuisine, served to you by the Z15. Or, actually catch your food in the fun 'launch it high' cabin!

TechnoPark, Silicon Town, Birmingham, just a skip away from Birmingham International Station (follow the holographic signs). Open every day all year round, from 10:00 to 20:00. Adults: £30. Children: £12.

Go to www.TechnoPark.Z1 for more details.

TechnoPark, the revolutionary adventure of tomorrow's world.

TASK:

Create a theme park and write a brochure that persuades people to visit it.

Explanation text

How an oxbow lake is formed

An oxbow lake is U-shaped, formed when a meandering river divides into a straighter streambed and leaves a reasonable amount of water that is surrounded by land.

Over a long time a mature river begins to curve more as the outside curve is eroded and sediment is deposited on the inside of the curve. There is centripetal force on the outside curve, which causes it to erode.

When the neck of the river erodes, sediment is deposited on the loop side of the stream, cutting it off, leaving a straighter river channel and an adjacent oxbow lake.

How to fly with Wonder Wings

Wonder Wings have been created so that humans can experience the sensation of independent flying. Once you have learnt to fly, you can fly for hours and the inbuilt satellite navigation will ensure you reach your destination efficiently.

Firstly, it is important to put on the protective wonder suit to which your wonder wings can be securely attached. Secondly, you need to ensure the blast battery is fully charged up. Thirdly, have a go in hover mode, with your body upright, not going too far off the ground or too fast. Once you have mastered hovering, put your wings in fly mode, push your body forward so that you move in horizontal mode, with stomach side parallel and facing the ground. Put your hands, with wings attached out to aid balancing and gliding. Gradually, as you build up your flying skills, you can speed up, increase your distance from the ground and go long distances.

If you are experiencing problems with learning to fly then enrol at a Wonder Wings school and you will be flying in no time.

Features of explanation text

- ❑ General statement of what is going to be explained
- ❑ Provide step-by-step detail in your explanation
- ❑ Use present tense
- ❑ Use technical vocabulary
- ❑ Use connectives.

TASK:

Write an explanation of 'How to look after a Zubzub' (which is a pretend bird with special powers).

Invitations and instructions

Pig number three

Has pleasure in inviting you to his

House Warming Party

On Saturday 17th September 2011

6.00pm to 8.00pm

At 3 Hampton Close

The Hamlet of Pigsbottom

Wolverhampton

Dress code: smart   *RSVP: 012342345*
                                        by 3rd September 2011

Please bring a bottle of pop   *By invitation only*

Any wolf look-alikes will be refused entry

Instructions for how to get there

Take a right out of Pigsbottom Station

Turn left on to Huff Lane

Walk for about 100 metres past Puff Pond

Turn right on to Hampton Close

You will find number 3 just after the piles of straw and sticks

Code of conduct

- Entry is by ringing the bell
- There will be no huffing or puffing
- There will be no sly jokes made about pigs

TASK:

Create an invitation to an event from one of your favourite stories and write a set of instructions of how to get there with a code of conduct.

Useful vocabulary: How? Verbs and corresponding adverbs:
to describe movement, speaking, seeing, eating and meeting

Movement verbs in past tense and suggested adverbs
advanced (tentatively)
ambled (nonchalantly)
approached (fearfully)
bounced (explosively)
bounded (energetically)
cantered (gracefully)
catapulted (gymnastically)
climbed (tirelessly)
clambered (precariously)
crawled (cautiously)
crept (warily)
danced (joyfully)
dashed (haphazardly)
edged (nervously)
fled (fearfully)

followed (faithfully)
glided (elegantly)
hobbled (bravely)
jogged (comfortably)
journeyed (hesitantly)
launched (dynamically)
limped (swiftly)
lunged (aggressively)
lurched (menacingly)
manoeuvred (expertly)
marched (purposefully)
meandered (peacefully)
paced (tearfully)
plodded (drearily)
prowled (suspiciously)
sauntered (casually)
scurried (briskly)

shuffled (arthritically)
skipped (ecstatically)
stepped (carefully)
stomped (grumpily)
strolled (leisurely)
strutted (sensationally)
stumbled (painfully)
staggered (gradually)
swaggered (clumsily)
swerved (dangerously)
trampled (recklessly)
traipsed (sulkily)
trekked (adventurously)
trudged (courageously)
waded (slowly)
waddled (gingerly)
wandered (foolishly)

Speaking verbs in past tense and suggested adverbs
agreed (definitively)
answered (defiantly)
argued (belligerently)
asserted (accusingly)
bellowed (thoughtlessly)
boasted (haughtily)
bragged (arrogantly)
challenged (provocatively)
chanted (joyously)
claimed (boastfully)
complained (predictably)
concluded (dismally)
confirmed (emphatically)

debated (frostily)
gasped (breathlessly)
growled (theatrically)
grunted (impulsively)
joked (jauntily)
hissed (spitefully)
howled (savagely)
moaned (monotonously)
noted (sympathetically)
pleaded (persuasively)
pledged (generously)
predicted (monumentally)
promised (antagonistically)
questioned (dispassionately)
quizzed (impatiently)

rejoiced (ecstatically)
reiterated (reproachfully)
remarked (stoically)
repeated (mundanely)
replied (emotionally)
said (eloquently)
sang (melodiously)
screeched (incredulously)
screamed (hysterically)
shouted (defensively)
wailed (spontaneously)
whimpered (pathetically)
whined (wistfully)
whispered (uncomfortably)
yelled (loudly)

Seeing verbs in past tense and suggested adverbs
gaped (gormlessly)
gawked (intrusively)
gazed (dreamily)
glanced (surreptitiously)
glared (indignantly)
glimpsed (momentarily)
identified (confidently)

investigated (thoroughly)
looked (benevolently)
noticed (guiltily)
observed (curiously)
perceived (indignantly)
perused (inquisitively)
recognised (instinctively)
regarded (adoringly)
scanned (carefully)

searched (anxiously)
scrutinized (pedantically)
spied (slyly)
stared (angrily)
surveyed (methodically)
viewed (meticulously)
visualised (excitedly)
watched (intermittently)
witnessed (unwillingly)

Eating verbs in past tense and suggested adverbs
annihilated (ruthlessly)
ate (covertly)
consumed (indifferently)
devoured (voraciously)
digested (abruptly)

diminished (fervently)
disposed (entirely)
feasted (ferociously)
fed (continuously)
gnawed (savagely)
gobbled (deliriously)
gorged (greedily)

gulped (hungrily)
savaged (sporadically)
scoffed (noisily)
sculpted (progressively)
slaughtered (savagely)
swallowed (contentedly)
wolfed (ravenously)

Meeting verbs in past tense and suggested adverbs
assembled (passively)
collided (coincidentally)
combined (inspiringly)

collaborated (secretively)
converged (purposefully)
embraced (awkwardly)
entwined (permanently)
met (memorably)

greeted (enthusiastically)
introduced (timidly)
joined (desperately)
rejoined (reluctantly)
welcomed (wholeheartedly)

Useful vocabulary: What? Adjectives: to describe nouns for people, creatures, cityscapes, landscapes, seascapes, seasons and the weather

People	(cowardly) instinct	(intriguing) scar	(portly) figure
(affable) soul	(cruel) humour	(involuntary) wink	(pretentious) boasts
(agitated) appearance	(dishevelled) garments	(lethargic) pace	(prominent) nose
(affirmative) nod	(distinct) freckles	(manicured) nails	(sarcastic) tongue
(arthritic) hobble	(distorted) memories	(materialistic) ambitions	(sullen) disposition
(astounding) hypocrisy	(exuberant) chatter	(melodious) voice	(theatrical) gestures
(authoritative) air	(flawless) facade	(mocking) grin	(trembling) hands
(awkward) fidget	(forlorn) figure	(muscular) torso	(offensive) remarks
(cantankerous) mood	(gaunt) features	(mysterious) past	(pallid) skin
(chic) lady	(gregarious) character	(nagging) temperament	(paranoid) accusations
(contagious) laugh	(glamorous) apparel	(narrow) lips	(rotund) face
(contemptuous) sneer	(haughty) tone	(outspoken) comments	(vague) wrinkles
(counterfeit) smile	(hostile) glare	(painful) limp	(vigorous) stride
(courageous) stoicism	(inquisitive) glance	(perturbed) eyebrows	(withered) arm

Creatures	(emaciated) frame	(incessant) twitch	(ruthless) brute
(breathless) excitement	(enchanting) skip	(ingenious) predator	(scaly) armour
(brisk) canter	(erratic) temper	(insatiable) appetite	(sharp) talons
(bulging) eyes	(excitable) nature	(lifeless) body	(silky) hide
(cacophonous) drone	(ferocious) growl	(loathsome) ogre	(slimy) skin
(conspicuous) spots	(flecked) fur	(magical) soar	(soothing) chant
(delicate) wings	(grumpy) frown	(persuasive) whimper	(snub) snout
(disgruntled) challenger	(hairy) beast	(plump) profile	(trembling) tail
(dominant) oppressor	(hefty) hind	(provocative) stance	(unkempt) hair
(eccentric) imaginings	(heinous) intentions	(repellant) odour	(vicious) claws
(elegant) launch	(humble) stoop	(repugnant) breath	(webbed) feet
(elfin) stature	(hypnotic) gaze	(resolute) roar	(wrinkled) coat

Cityscapes	(destitute) vagrant	(impatient) traffic	(roaming) litter
(anonymous) alleys	(dismal) sky	(intimidating) skyscraper	(shrill) brakes
(barking) motorbikes	(dominated) houses	(mumbling) cars	(smoking) exhausts
(bellowing) lorries	(earnest) pedestrians	(polished) mall	(stuttering) trains
(bossy) lights	(elaborate) decorations	(premeditated) parks	(territorial) fences
(cavernous) holes	(exhausted) buses	(pungent) pollution	(tongue-tied) bicycles
(contemplative) shopper	(grandiose) museum	(regurgitating) bins	(pummelled) roads
(credible) gossip	(harmonious) market	(reflective) windows	(truculent) crowds
(derelict) warehouse	(hungry) dustcarts	(reliable) clock	(vibrating) roadworks

Landscapes and seascapes	(decomposing) planks	(hectic) rockpools	(rickety) fence
(abundant) foliage	(decrepit) bridge	(inaccessible) trail	(obstructive) bushes
(ancient) rumours	(dense) growth	(lonely) track	(plummeting) dunes
(antagonistic) cold	(dilapidated) ruin	(majestic) ruin	(rustling) fields
(cascading) waterfall	(diminutive) steps	(marauding) cows	(secretive) caves
(chaotic) brambles	(embossed) pebbles	(mellow) streams	(scattered) villages
(cobbled) incline	(feisty) waves	(mesmerizing) ripples	(signed) sand
(crooked) tree	(flickering) forest	(mountainous) terrain	(stoic) stones
(crumbling) walls	(frantic) flies	(outstretched) beach	(surging) hills
(crunchy) sticks	(frenzied) river	(precarious) rocks	(tickling) grass
	(gregarious) seagulls	(ramshackle) cottage	(undulating) valleys

Seasons and weather	(dynamic) Spring	(hopeful) saplings	(snowy) coat
(aggressive) sleet	(eerie) darkness	(inhospitable) Winter	(speckled) light
(auburn) Autumn	(ethereal) rainbow	(intense) sun	(spiteful) rain
(blustery) clouds	(fickle) wind	(malevolent) monsoon	(threatening) lightning
(crashing) thunder	(foggy) confusion	(monotonous) fog	(unblemished) ice
(crisp) leaves	(furry) snow	(shimmering) Summer	(whispering) breeze

Descriptive text: Checklist

Aim: entertain/inform by conveying a strong and interesting sensory image. *Is this aim fulfilled?*

Success criteria for 'what makes good writing'	Success criteria for 'what makes good descriptive writing'
Does the text involve good ideas?	Is more than one of object, setting, person or event described?
Are ambitious/technical vocabulary/phrases used?	Is there logical movement around what is described?
Are sentences varied?	Is detailed description used, including imperfections, with a sense of mystery or emotion, possibly via rumour?
Is punctuation used accurately?	Are poetic devices used, like similes, personification, themes?
Is text organised in paragraphs?	Is description from the senses?
Do ideas logically link?	
Do a range of openers/connectives support text flow?	
Is enough relevant information included?	

Narrative text: Checklist

Aim: entertain by telling an exciting story or persuade by telling a story with a moral. *Is this aim fulfilled?*

Success criteria for 'what makes good writing'	Success criteria for 'what makes good narrative writing'
Does the text involve good ideas?	Does the narrative start with action?
Are ambitious/technical vocabulary/phrases used?	Is the main character introduced quickly?
Are sentences varied?	Is the setting introduced quickly?
Is punctuation used accurately?	Is the dilemma introduced quickly?
Is text organised in paragraphs?	Does the narrative use cliffhangers?
Do ideas logically link?	Does the narrative maintain the reader's interest?
Do a range of openers/connectives support text flow?	Does the main character develop?
Is enough relevant information included?	Does the action build to a satisfactory resolution that links to previous action?

Formal letter writing: Checklist

Aim: inform/persuade by providing required detail, that is well organised. *Is this aim fulfilled?*

Success criteria for 'what makes good writing'	Success criteria for 'what makes good formal letter writing'
Does the text involve good ideas?	Are letter format for addresses and date used?
Are ambitious/technical vocabulary/phrases used?	Are conventions for opening and closing used? That is: Dear (named person) – close with Yours sincerely or Dear Sir/ Madam – close with Yours faithfully
Are sentences varied?	Does the opening paragraph state reason of writing?
Is punctuation used accurately?	Does the next paragraph/s provide detailed, though concise information?
Is text organised in paragraphs?	Does the final paragraph state what you want to happen?
Do ideas logically link?	Is a formal and factual tone used?
Do a range of openers/connectives support text flow?	Are the appropriate tenses used – such as past tense to recount and future tense for what should happen?
Is enough relevant information included?	Is first person used?

Play script: Checklist

Aim: entertain/inform/persuade by exciting monologue or dialogue from an interesting character or characters. *Is this aim fulfilled?*

Success criteria for 'what makes good writing'	Success criteria for 'what makes good play script writing'
Does the text involve good ideas?	Does the text have a title, cast list and setting?
Are ambitious/technical vocabulary/phrases used?	Are the characters names set in a margin?
Are sentences varied?	Are character and stage present tense directions in brackets?
Is punctuation used accurately?	Are new lines used for each new speaker?
Is text organised in paragraphs?	
Do ideas logically link?	
Do a range of openers/connectives support text flow?	
Is enough relevant information included?	

Diary writing: Checklist

Aim: entertain/inform by providing an interesting personal account and viewpoint. *Is this aim fulfilled?*

Success criteria for 'what makes good writing'	Success criteria for 'what makes good diary writing'
Does the text involve good ideas?	Are only key and interesting events recounted?
Are ambitious/technical vocabulary/phrases used?	Is a chronological order, along with temporal connectives, used?
Are sentences varied?	Are descriptive and emotive vocabulary used?
Is punctuation used accurately?	Is the entry written in the first person?
Is text organised in paragraphs?	Is there a lead in orientation line/paragraph?
Do ideas logically link?	Are personal viewpoints conveyed that show the emotion and personality of the writer?
Do a range of openers/connectives support text flow?	Is there a closing statement?
Is enough relevant information included?	Is a 'chatty' (personal) style used?

Autobiographical/Biographical text: Checklist

Aim: entertain/inform by providing an interesting account. *Is this aim fulfilled?*

Success criteria for 'what makes good writing'	Success criteria for 'what makes good autobiographical/biographical writing'
Does the text involve good ideas?	Is the text written in first person (autobiographical text) or third person (biographical text)?
Are ambitious/technical vocabulary/phrases used?	Does it contain interesting information?
Are sentences varied?	After an orientation line/paragraph, is the text organised in chronological order, with chunks of information per paragraph for certain periods of life?
Is punctuation used accurately?	Does the reorientation paragraph sum up or look forward?
Is text organised in paragraphs?	Is it mostly written in past tense until looking forward?
Do ideas logically link?	Does the text reveal the life and character of the subject in an engaging fashion?
Do a range of openers/connectives support text flow?	
Is enough relevant information included?	

Report/Non-chronological report writing: Checklist

Aim: entertain/inform/persuade by providing required factual detail, that is well organised. *Is this aim fulfilled?*

Success criteria for 'what makes good writing'	Success criteria for 'what makes good report writing'
Does the text involve good ideas?	Is the report, whether it is about an historical event (chronological) or a non-chronological report (so does not depend on a time order), well organised?
Are ambitious/technical vocabulary/phrases used?	Although paragraphs are not titled, do they start with topic sentences that show what the paragraph will be about?
Are sentences varied?	Is language formal, using topical/technical vocabulary?
Is punctuation used accurately?	Is information factual or made to sound factual?
Is text organised in paragraphs?	Is the text detailed and interesting?
Do ideas logically link?	Is the report usually in present tense (not historical) and in the third person?
Do a range of openers/connectives support text flow?	Does the orientation line/paragraph indicate what is to be written about?
Is enough relevant information included?	Does the reorientation paragraph sum up, show the impact or look forward to the future of the subject?

Newspaper report writing: Checklist

Aim: entertain/inform/persuade by providing required factual detail, that is well organised. *Is this aim fulfilled?*

Success criteria for 'what makes good writing'	Success criteria for 'what makes good newspaper report writing'
Does the text involve good ideas?	Is a relevant, interesting and concise headline used?
Are ambitious/technical vocabulary/phrases used?	Does an orientation line, a complex sentence, show who, what, where, when, why and how to interest?
Are sentences varied?	Is an opening paragraph used that provides more detail to the orientation?
Is punctuation used accurately?	Is further factual detail, in past tense, built up before quotations from key characters?
Is text organised in paragraphs?	Does a re-orientation line/paragraph bring the reader up to date or look to the future?
Do ideas logically link?	Is formal language used?
Do a range of openers/connectives support text flow?	Is the article mostly written in the past tense?
Is enough relevant information included?	Is the article written in the third person?

Witness report writing: Checklist

Aim: inform by providing extensive chronological detail. *Is this aim fulfilled?*

Success criteria for 'what makes good writing'	Success criteria for 'what makes good witness report writing'
Does the text involve good ideas?	Is there a chronological order to the recount of events?
Are ambitious/technical vocabulary/phrases used?	Is description of events detailed?
Are sentences varied?	Is the report in first person?
Is punctuation used accurately?	Is the report factual?
Is text organised in paragraphs?	
Do ideas logically link?	
Do a range of openers/connectives support text flow?	
Is enough relevant information included?	

Adverts: Checklist

Aim: entertain/persuade by informing an audience of the merits of a product, service or campaign. *Is this aim fulfilled?*

Success criteria for 'what makes good writing'	Success criteria for 'what makes good advert writing'
Does the text involve good ideas?	Are the benefits highlighted to show how life will be improved with the purchase or change?
Are ambitious/technical vocabulary/phrases used?	Are questions used to link the benefits directly to the audience by involving them?
Are sentences varied?	Is the text organised by name, lead question, benefits, other crucial information and slogan?
Is punctuation used accurately?	Is the language persuasive, with positive adjectives and a catchy slogan?
Is text organised in paragraphs?	Is positive opinion made to sound like fact?
Do ideas logically link?	
Do a range of openers/connectives support text flow?	
Is enough relevant information included?	

Two-sided argument: Checklist

Aim: persuade by informing an audience of different points of view with a conclusion. *Is this aim fulfilled?*

Success criteria for 'what makes good writing'	Success criteria for 'what makes good two-sided argument writing'
Does the text involve good ideas?	Is the task turned into a question to be answered?
Are ambitious/technical vocabulary/phrases used?	Does the introduction define the question's key parts?
Are sentences varied?	Are several arguments given against your view?
Is punctuation used accurately?	Are several arguments given for your view?
Is text organised in paragraphs?	Does a conclusion provide a final view (perhaps a compromise) answer the question?
Do ideas logically link?	Is the argument written in present tense?
Do a range of openers/connectives support text flow?	Are temporal connectives, such as first and finally, used?
Is enough relevant information included?	Does the argument sound factual and authoritative?

Persuasive leaflet: Checklist

Aim: inform and persuade by relevant, well organised information about a product, service or campaign. *Is this aim fulfilled?*

Success criteria for 'what makes good writing'	Success criteria for 'what makes good persuasive leaflet writing'
Does the text involve good ideas?	Does the opening paragraph introduce who, what, where, when, and why under a general heading?
Are ambitious/technical vocabulary/phrases used?	Are subtitles used to show what aspect is covered in each paragraph?
Are sentences varied?	Are bullet points used for clarity?
Is punctuation used accurately?	Is all the required information included that will persuade the reader why and how to act?
Is text organised in paragraphs?	Is a final catchy, persuasive slogan used?
Do ideas logically link?	Is the leaflet in present tense?
Do a range of openers/connectives support text flow?	Is the leaflet in second person?
Is enough relevant information included?	

Explanation text: Checklist

Aim: inform by relevant, well-ordered information of occurrence. *Is this aim fulfilled?*

Success criteria for 'what makes good writing'	Success criteria for 'what makes good explanation writing'
Does the text involve good ideas?	Is there a title that shows what the text explains?
Are ambitious/technical vocabulary/phrases used?	Is there a general statement of what is going to be explained?
Are sentences varied?	Is there a step-by-step explanation?
Is punctuation used accurately?	Is present tense used?
Is text organised in paragraphs?	Is technical vocabulary used?
Do ideas logically link?	
Do a range of openers/connectives support text flow?	
Is enough relevant information included?	

Invitations: Checklist

Aim: inform by concise, well-ordered information of who, what, where, when, why and how. *Is this aim fulfilled?*

Success criteria for 'what makes good writing'	Success criteria for 'what makes good invitation writing'
Does the text involve good ideas?	Is all the relevant who, what, where, when and why included?
Are ambitious/technical vocabulary/phrases used?	Is the invitation clearly set out in lines?
Are sentences varied?	Would the reader know how to reply, how to dress and what to bring?
Is punctuation used accurately?	
Is text organised in paragraphs?	
Do ideas logically link?	
Do a range of openers/connectives support text flow?	
Is enough relevant information included?	

Instructions: Checklist

Aim: inform by concise, well-ordered information, with instructions, of how to act, create or participate. *Is this aim fulfilled?*

Success criteria for 'what makes good writing'	Success criteria for 'what makes good instructions'
Does the text involve good ideas?	Does the text have a heading that shows the aim of the text?
Are ambitious/technical vocabulary/phrases used?	Is the information usefully split, with headings, such as tools and directions?
Are sentences varied?	Are bullet points or numbers used to provide clarity?
Is punctuation used accurately?	Is text in an order to fulfil its aim?
Is text organised in paragraphs?	Is the text in second person?
Do ideas logically link?	Are imperatives used?
Do a range of openers/connectives support text flow?	Is present tense used?
Is enough relevant information included?	

Booster Projects: Oliver Island

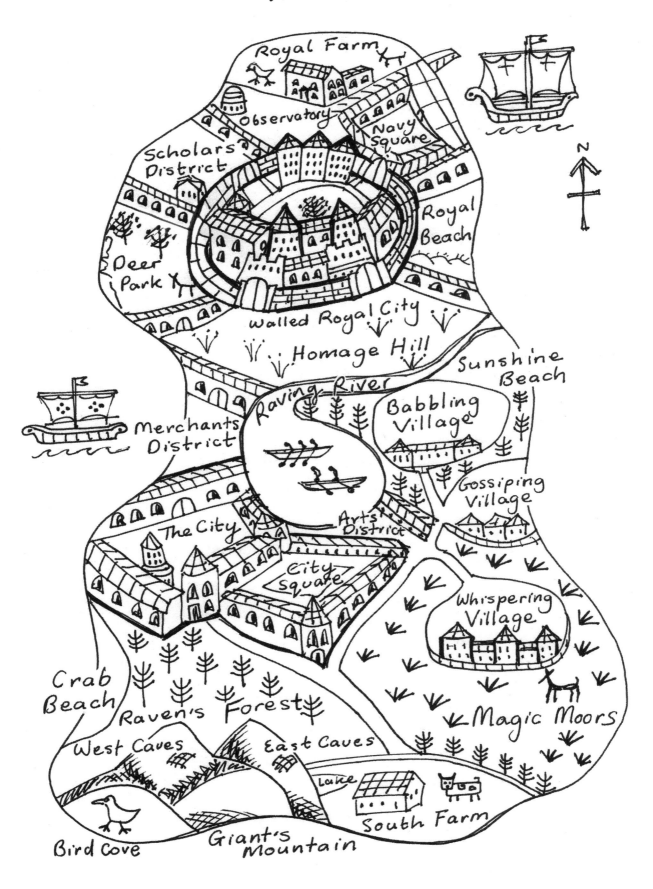

Oliver Island: Booster projects to support the understanding of what makes good writing

Six two-hour projects are organised as:

Project 1 – Comprehension and vocabulary

- ❑ What I know about writing well
- ❑ Read and analyse the Quest Story, 'The Battle to find Dr Joseph', with comprehension questions, answers and analysis of answers
- ❑ Useful vocabulary for quest stories: prepositions, connectives, adjectives, nouns, verbs and adverbs, adjectives with nouns and verbs with adverbs

Project 2 – Sentences, punctuation and style

- ❑ Recognise simple sentences and the use of the full stop, question mark, exclamation mark, ellipses or closing speech marks
- ❑ Turn simple into compound sentences by adding another main clause after a co-ordinating conjunction or semi-colon
- ❑ Turn simple into complex sentences by adding subordinate information with commas, dashes or parentheses
- ❑ Recognise compound-complex sentences that use conjunctions or a semi-colon between two main clauses and further include subordinate information.
- ❑ Upgrade sentences by using adjectives to describe nouns and adverbs to describe verbs, with or without similes
- ❑ Use apostrophes
- ❑ Upgrade text by asking who, what, where, when, why, which and how questions and using the useful vocabulary list for quest stories

Project 3 – Paragraphs of description

- ❑ Analyse description to find out what makes it good, using the descriptive writing analysis sheet to mark *The King's Room*
- ❑ Describe scenes in paragraphs, with people, events and objects, using ambitious vocabulary, poetic devices, sensory description, a sense of history or viewpoint and suspense

Project 4 – Entertaining text

- ❑ What makes good writing?
- ❑ Assess the narrative, *The Battle to find Dr Joseph,* based on 'what makes good writing?' and 'what makes good story writing?'
- ❑ Assess and edit *The Apprentice* to the success criteria for 'what makes good writing?' and 'what makes good story writing?'

Project 5 – Instructions and information text

- ❑ Create instructions for how to reach Dr Joseph
- ❑ Create information text about Oliver Island with respect to 'what makes good non-chronological report writing'

Project 6 – Persuasive text

- ❑ Names and slogans warm up: write names and slogans that give memory and appeal to a product, brand or campaign
- ❑ Assess a radio advert for the Oliver Island Museum using an analysis grid of success criteria for writing adverts
- ❑ Plan, create and edit a radio advert that persuades visitors to 'The Royal Palace' on Oliver Island using the success criteria for an advert with the overall aim to persuade
- ❑ What I know about writing well to show the learning from the whole project

Project 1– Comprehension and vocabulary

What I know about writing well

Create a spidergram to show what you know about writing well.

What I know about writing well

The Battle to find Dr Joseph

Throwing down the gauntlet

When Oliver Island was on the point of civil war due to King Matlock having treated its citizens so poorly, his twin brother, Riley (born just twenty minutes later than him) decided to have him imprisoned so that he would learn humility and become a greater king. Matlock escaped into the night to find his cousin, Dr Joseph, a very talented engineer, to commission the design and creation of an advanced weapon that would wipe out the whole of the walled Royal City that had now been taken over by Riley and his entourage. Riley, on hearing his brother's intentions, decided to get to Dr Joseph first. The wise scientist went into hiding, somewhere on Giant's Mountain, and the desperate battle to find Dr Joseph began…

The quest to find Dr Joseph

Frantically, Matlock descended through the unruly, spitefully thorny and steep terrain of Homage Hill. He was inadequately clothed in a short sleeved top, lightweight cotton trousers and thin-soled shoes. By the time he had reached the bottom of the valley, his skin was ripped, as if torn by the claws of a ferocious animal, and blood trickled down his exposed arms, but he did not notice for he was focused on the heavy breathing and intermittent growling of the dogs that were chasing him, followed by the Palace Guards, who were hacking into the overgrown territory with sharp swords. As darkness was no protection from the sniffing, snarling beasts, the King leapt into the dangerous, turbulent waters of Raving River to escape them.

Matlock twisted uncontrollably into the jagged stones and spiky branches along the water's edge as the swift, bellowing and icy-cold water thrust him around savagely. Strangely, he just noted how desperately frozen he was, as if he could not acknowledge the complete drama that was unfolding. He had never been cold before. The memory of a homeless man, whom he had ordered to be removed from just outside the palace gates a few weeks before, flashed into his head – that man had actually looked blue with cold. How dare these people get in one's way! A violent collision with a malicious rock finally knocked the royal into unconscious oblivion; he was open mouthed, taking in the water and sinking to the murky depths of the riverbed.

A clatter of a pan on the grill of an open fire woke Matlock. He now wore only shorts beneath a coarse blanket that itched his bruised and aching torso, like fleas on a dog. He was on some pathetically emaciated mattress within a small scullery that smelt of fresh fish and from the room beyond he could hear the low voices and laughter of a man and a woman. As he sat up, he winced in agony. He held his head in his hands; he had no memory of how he had reached this domicile. He knew there would be a substantial reward for his return to the Royal Dungeons. So, he could trust no one. He must leave immediately. But as he surveyed a narrow window, the door opened and in walked a woman, about mid-thirties, wearing a friendly smile. "How are you doing, young man?" she enquired. "I'm Martha, and my husband, Samuel, saved you from drowning last night." Then, a well built man, presumably Samuel, loomed up behind Martha in the doorway, with a broad smile that matched his wife's.

"Thank you," uttered Matlock, narrowing his eyes with suspicion as he waited for the couple to pounce on him and present him to Riley or demand money from him for saving him and taking him in.

"You're welcome," answered Samuel, with a deep booming voice. "You are lucky I went fishing last night. Now I will leave Martha to get you what you need, as I have to get to work."

As the door slammed, Matlock assumed that Samuel was off to alert Riley of his whereabouts. "Off to get his reward is he? They will fine you out of your home for fishing illegally and stealing the King's fish."

Martha looked confused. "My husband saved your life, we gave you a bed and you are threatening us? I will feed you breakfast and then I want you out of here. We are not thieves for living on what is naturally there and we could easily starve on what my husband earns as a woodcutter."

"Do you know who I am?" shouted Matlock.

Martha glared at him. "Someone who is lucky to be alive," she pronounced angrily. "Or perhaps not!" she muttered, as she left the room. She returned to the room with some clothes. "These were my brother's things prior to his recent death – I think they should fit you," she said, before promptly leaving.

Matlock dressed in the baggy cloth trousers, shirt and tunic. He then went into the front room. Martha was sat down. "The last of the fish is for you," she urged, pushing a plate to the opposite side of the table, before indicating to Matlock to take a seat.

Matlock consumed the fish, hungrily, while looking around the tiny room that managed to host another unsubstantial mattress, table and just two wooden chairs. The walls were crumbling from neglect and one windowpane did not meet its surround and was letting in cold air in spite of the roaring fire. People actually lived like this? A line of ants rummaged around the floor by his feet. Disgusting!

"Your shoes are dry now," asserted Martha as she fetched them from the edge of the log fire and presented them to Matlock.

"So what reward do you want?" asked the King, with genuine curiosity.

"Our reward was to help you and you thanked us already," answered Martha, coldly, with apparent resentment.

Matlock, breathed in through enlarged nostrils and then puffed out his chest haughtily, believing he was too good to be spoken to in such a manner. In fact, it was her duty to put his needs first! "Do you really not know who I am?" he asked, with a sudden need to assert his status.

"I thought you were a man in need, but not a very nice man it turns out. Perhaps you don't need to be nice when you are a king!" replied Martha, defiantly.

Matlock gasped for he had never been spoken to so offensively. "You are nothing," he screamed. "You live in a hovel, in total squalor. You are a peasant!"

"We live, Sir, in laughter and love," shouted Martha. "You don't need jewels to be happy in life. You think you are great because of what you were born to? Great men and women care for the rest of mankind and learn how to create true harmony for those around them or they are worth less than the ants on my floor. Now get out of my home."

The morning mist afforded the King some cover until he reached Raven's Forest. Dense canopy provided a comforting darkness along a distinct, though overgrown track to Crystal Cottage. Matlock had been here several times before, when he needed advice on important state matters. A little behind him, the careless breaking of a twig in some dense foliage, spooked the unpopular royal and he momentarily froze like a cornered rabbit about to be attacked. Perhaps it was just a forest creature? Another crack of wood debris in the same location, suggested someone was there. He desperately bolted to the remote cottage. He knocked at the door, urgently, and hurried in.

Crystal had long, grey, unkempt hair that untidily framed her surprisingly young and pretty face. "I've been expecting you, King Matlock," she quietly asserted, without redirecting her gaze from a set of crystal shapes on her table. They were arranged in an order that appeared to mimic the landmarks of the island.

Matlock sat opposite Crystal. "I need your help," he urged, just audibly. "My brother imprisoned me in the Royal Dungeons and I escaped. I now need to find my cousin so that I can kill Riley and re-establish myself."

"No one escapes from the Royal Dungeons, not even the rats," considered Crystal. "Someone must have deliberately helped you. As for your cousin – let me think." Crystal closed her eyes and her hands drifted slowly across her arrangement of gems, until they settled on the largest one. There seems to be good energy coming from Giant's Mountain, from the West Caves. Dr Joseph is there. You will be fine." Crystal opened her eyes.

"You are the only person in the world who makes me feel alright," stated Matlock, with unusual gratitude. "Why?"

"I feel what is to come. You will find true greatness," answered Crystal, her eyes now meeting with his. She smiled.

Matlock did not question her statement; he assumed it meant that he would get a weapon and defeat all of his enemies and rule his kingdom with rigorous control.

A strange breeze in the cottage gave a weird distortion to the objects in his view. "Is this some kind of magic?" asked the King, confused.

Crystal held her hand out, grabbed something and her fingers were suddenly partly missing.

"What is this trickery?" questioned Matlock, alarmed.

"It is my camouflage cloth. It is made of special reflective microscopic fibres which simply reflect the environment, so that there is apparent invisibility."

"This would be most useful for a fugitive!"

"It is not enough to cover you," answered Crystal, reluctant to lend him her most recent creation.

"I will return it to you as soon as I can. I promise," urged Matlock.

Matlock was in an unrecognisable state when he reached near to the summit of Giant's Mountain. His dark hair was lightened with the dust that had dispersed as he scrambled up. He was bedraggled, sweaty and trying not to breathe too heavily. If anyone saw him now, they would think he were a peasant, especially as he wore Martha's brother's sack-like clothes. Surely, man was more than his clothes? An extremely strange thought entered the King's head – what made him better than anyone else? And then, rather shockingly, Martha's voice came into his head to stir him up further: "You think you are great because of what you were born to?" How dare a peasant question the King's position. This was treason; Martha must die!

Movement ahead of the King brought Matlock back to the moment. There, about twenty metres ahead of him, stood one of the Palace Guards. How strange that his cousin should have protection. Dr Joseph had never been interested in being a celebrated royal and did not enjoy all its paraphernalia and yet there was a guard with a sword clutched in his hand.

Matlock slid his right hand into his pocket, pulling out the camouflage cloth, which he placed over his head. He walked, tentatively, towards the guard. To the sentry, a headless man seemingly approached and, in terror, he dropped his blade and raced away. The King picked up the sword, replaced the cloth in his pocket and advanced to the cave.

Finale

"My dear cousin," shouted Matlock, as he entered the cave. "I need you to design and build me the most amazing weapon that will bring down my treacherous brother."

Dr Joseph, who was busy polishing a metallic box in dim candlelight, looked at Matlock. "No," he stated, emphatically. "Your brother is also my cousin and this foolishness must stop right now."

"He started this fight," stated Matlock, tensely, "and I am the King."

"There are no winners in war," Joseph answered, emphatically.

"Those with the greatest weapons always win," contested Matlock.

"No. Go away. You will kill your brother and destroy many lives."

"Starting with yours if you don't help me," promised Matlock, angrily, as he flung the sword blade across his cousin's throat.

"Put the sword down, Matlock and I will show you how you can win back your kingdom," gasped Joseph.

Matlock looked at the earnest eyes of Joseph, gave a minimal nod and put his sword onto the uneven cave floor.

"Now sit down," demanded the engineer, more calmly. "There you go – that's how you do it!"

"I don't understand," the King said, with baffled eyebrows.

"I just disarmed you with words. You had your sword around my neck and you are now sat here with me. Speech is the greatest tool in the World. Talk to your brother.

You know him and you can appeal to him and persuade him how you can work together to provide a harmonious community without the spilling of blood. Once upon a time you played together around this great island and everyone loved you as they loved your father, the great King Oliver before you. Today, people just despise, perhaps even pity you. This island needs the two of you to lead them with intelligence, strength and compassion."

"It seems I have had a wasted journey!" remarked Matlock, irately.

"Really? Did you not learn anything on your trek to find me?"

Matlock put his head in his hands. He looked down to his shoes and there by his feet were a line of ants, working together.

"Oh!" said Matlock, after a while. "I am worth less than the ants! Look how they work together! I must find Riley and make our island great once more. I must find him."

From the shadows at the back of the cave, Riley moved forward. Matlock was open mouthed with surprise. Eventually he noted, "So, the Palace Guard was for you." He stood up and met Riley. "I have been such a fool!"

"You have had quite a journey, my dear brother," stated Riley. "We were terrified you would drown."

"I don't understand", answered Matlock. Then with sudden realisation he blurted, "You were watching me escape? You had me followed?"

"Of course, we wanted to make sure you were safe! You have been followed since you left the palace."

"Does Samuel work for you?"

"No. He saved you like a true hero. He risked his life for yours."

"So, he and his wife, Martha, are for real? It doesn't make sense. They had the chance for more because they could have turned me in or asked me for a reward, but they didn't. They were just happy to help a fellow human! When I was rude, they gave me their last mouthful of fish. Brother, they are happy with nothing, but deserve everything. No… in fact they have it all," concluded Matlock, with sudden understanding, awe and humility. "That is true greatness!"

"Well young Matlock," said Dr Riley, "now you really do deserve to be the King!"

The Battle to find Dr Joseph: comprehension questions

Questions	Answers	Analysis
What is the name of the King's cousin? (1 mark)		I can answer retrieval questions *or* I need to read more and understand what is happening in text
How does Samuel help Matlock? (1 mark)		I can answer retrieval questions *or* I need to read more and understand what is happening in text
What does Matlock take from Crystal that he believes will help him? (1 mark)		I can answer retrieval questions *or* I need to read more and understand what is happening in text
What does Martha think of Matlock? Refer to the text to support your answer. (2 marks – for 2 points, each with reference to the narrative.)		I can answer inference questions *or* I need to read higher level text and practise working out what an author suggests from what is written
What is the purpose of the ants in this text? (2 marks)		I can answer inference questions *or* I need to read higher level text and practise working out what an author suggests from what is written
What two journeys could the King be said to have gone on in this narrative? (2 marks)		I can answer inference questions *or* I need to read higher level text and practise working out what an author suggests from what is written
Write four words from the second paragraph that give a sense of sound. (1 mark)		I can answer stylistic questions *or* I need to learn more about vocabulary choice *or* genre *or* the layout of text
'*He knocked at the door, urgently.*' What does the addition of the adverb do for the sense of this sentence? (2 marks)		I can answer stylistic questions *or* I need to learn more about vocabulary choice *or* genre *or* the layout of text

The Battle to find Dr Joseph: comprehension answers and analysis

Questions	Answers	Analysis
What is the name of the King's cousin? (1 mark)	Dr Joseph	I can answer retrieval questions *or* I need to read more and understand what is happening in text
How does Samuel help Matlock? (1 mark)	He saves his life *or* He saves him from drowning *or* He puts him up in his home	I can answer retrieval questions *or* I need to read more and understand what is happening in text
What does Matlock take from Crystal that he believes will help him? (1 mark)	The camouflage cloth	I can answer retrieval questions *or* I need to read more and understand what is happening in text
What does Martha think of Matlock? Refer to the text to support your answer. (2 marks – for 2 points, each with a reference to the narrative.)	Martha does not like Matlock as she tells him, "*…I want you out of here.*" Martha pities Matlock as she thinks maybe he is not lucky to be alive ("*…perhaps not!*") Martha thinks Matlock is not very nice as she says "*Perhaps you don't need to be nice when you are a king!*"	I can answer inference questions *or* I need to read higher level text and practise working out what an author suggests from what is written
What is the purpose of the ants in this text? (2 marks)	The first time Matlock sees the ants is when Martha questions his values. The second time they perhaps remind him of the first time and he sees them '*working together without prejudice*' and this seems to accompany his realisation that he has previously been a fool and needs to work for the common good.	I can answer inference questions *or* I need to read higher level text and practise working out what an author suggests from what is written
What two journeys could the King be said to have gone on in this narrative? (2 marks)	The King journeys to find his cousin, Dr Joseph. He also goes on a personal journey and gains an understanding of true greatness.	I can answer inference questions *or* I need to read higher level text and practise working out what an author suggests from what is written
Write four words from the second paragraph that give a sense of sound. (1 mark)	*breathing, growling, hacking, sniffing, snarling, turbulent, bellowing, collision , knocked*	I can answer stylistic questions *or* I need to learn more about vocabulary choice *or* genre *or* the layout of text
'*He knocked at the door, urgently.*' What does the addition of the adverb do for the sense of this sentence? (2 marks)	*Urgently* is the adverb that describes how he knocks at the door. It gives a sense of desperation because the King has been spooked.	I can answer stylistic questions *or* I need to learn more about vocabulary choice *or* genre *or* the layout of text

The Battle to find Dr Joseph: vocabulary for quest stories

Use the narrative, dictionary and thesaurus to identify useful prepositions, connectives, adjectives, nouns, verbs and adverbs, adjectives with nouns and verbs with adverbs that can be used in quest stories.

Prepositions (words that support the where, when, how and why of a sentence, like: *above, after, with, since*).	
Connectives (words that give logic to text, like: *also, however, consequently, firstly, meanwhile*).	
Adjectives (words that describe nouns or pronouns, like: *murky, dank and muffled*).	
Nouns or pronouns (words that name, like: *mountain, clock, he, they, which*).	
Verbs (action words like: *observe, bounce, attack*)	
Adverbs (words that describe verbs like: *angrily, timidly, savagely*).	
Adjectives with nouns like: *sinister clouds, icy water, emaciated horse.*	
Verbs with adverbs like: *approaching cautiously, raining ferociously, gawking menacingly.*	

Project 2 – The Battle to find Dr Joseph: sentences, punctuation and style from the narrative

Write down the punctuation that you find to end sentences.	
Copy a simple sentence from the narrative. Annotate it to show the subject (noun) and what is said about the subject (verb). Underline the extra words that are required to make it complete.	
Copy a compound sentence from the narrative. Underline the co-ordinating conjunction or semi-colon that connects the two main clauses. Write down other co-ordinating conjunctions (the words that join two main clauses).	
Copy a complex sentence from the narrative. Underline the subordinate clause (the extra information that cannot stand by itself as a sentence). What punctuation is required to add subordinate information?	
Copy a simple sentence and add another main clause to turn it into a compound sentence, with a co-ordinating conjunction or a semi-colon.	
Copy a simple sentence and add subordinate information to make it into a complex sentence, with a comma or commas, dash or parentheses.	
Copy a compound-complex sentence, which has two main clauses and subordinate information.	
Copy a simple sentence. Add an adjective, adverb and extra information to the sentence.	
Copy a simple sentence. Add an adjective, adverb and extra information to the sentence. Use a thesaurus to upgrade some of the vocabulary.	
Copy a simple sentence. Add an adjective, adverb and extra information to the sentence. Use a thesaurus to upgrade some of the vocabulary. Also, use sensory description and make a comparison with a simile.	

Using apostrophes

Copy out or create some sentences that use apostrophes because something belongs to something else, like *The creature's dinner…* (dinner belonging to one creature) or *The creatures' dinner…* (dinner belonging to more than one creature).	
Shorten these sets of two words into one with an apostrophe to replace a letter: do not, would not, are not, you are, they are, it is, she is, he is.	
Understand that the exception to the apostrophe rule is it's which means it is. So *its dinner* does not include an apostrophe for possession. Write out some sentences that contain it's and its.	
Understand that plural nouns that don't have something belonging do not use apostrophes, like *The creatures were hungry*. Write out some sentences that use plurals without apostrophes.	

Upgrading text by asking *what, how, who, where, when, why, which, how* questions and using the useful vocabulary list and thesaurus

The King leapt into the river.

The (*what?*) King leapt (*how?*), (*what? who? where? when? why? which? or how?*)

The terrified King leapt athletically into the ice-cold river to escape the snarling, sniffing beasts.

The water flowed rapidly.

The turbulent water flowed rapidly, violently smashing the helpless man against the jagged river's edge, which ripped into his skin like a ferocious tiger.

Upgrade these sentences by asking relevant questions that will stimulate a range of sentences with interesting detail and description

The King walked down the road.

His footsteps echoed.

He was petrified.

He headed towards the forest.

Upgrade the following passage by using the useful vocabulary lists (pages 40 and 41), a thesaurus and asking relevant questions that will stimulate a range of sentences with interesting detail and description

The King began to climb Giant's Mountain. It was dark. He was cold. He scrambled up the rock face. He felt there was something behind him. As the wind blew, he clung on. It was a while before he reached the summit.

Project 3 – Paragraphs of description

The King's Room

Luxurious gold, silky paper adorned the walls of the King's spacious chamber. In the centre of the white, square, panelled ceiling a grand, crystal chandelier hung down, producing symmetrical light specks on the sumptuous and immense, moon-cream carpet.

An oak four-poster bed dominated the opposite side of the room to white painted double doors. Heavy, red velvet drapes closed the vast bed in darkness. The red velvet was repeated in the closed curtains that kept the early evening light out to both sides of the bed. Another wall hosted a large carved wooden framed oil portrait (a distant ancestor to the King). A chubby face, burdened with a long bony nose and strangely dark, bulging eyes, all framed by straight, drab and dark hair, stared down on to a cold, white marble bureau, which was intricately decorated with gold, floral edging, fancy curved feet and shell handles and upon it a red leather diary lay, open. Across its centre pages, in slanted dark writing, lay the secrets of the King. Why had the King recently commissioned another ship? Was war looming? What was the King thinking? Should royalty really write diaries?

Mona moved gently across to the book, with avid curiosity, a primrose scent lingering behind her. She did not have a chubby face, burdened with a long bony nose and strangely dark, bulging eyes. As she read the King's words, she stifled a content giggle with hand over her petite mouth. He was not writing about war. He was writing about her!

Analysis of descriptive writing

Success criteria	Analysis via commentary
Does the text use ambitious vocabulary, including relevant adjectives and adverbs?	
Is a range of sentences used, with relevant punctuation?	
Does the text use description from the senses?	
Are poetic devices used?	
Is suspense built up or a sense of history given to the subject or a view of what characters in the description think of what is described?	
Is the description of more than one of: settings, people, objects and events, put together for added interest?	
Is movement of a character around the scene or other means used to aid the description in an interesting way?	
Is a vivid picture conveyed, including any imperfections?	
Is the text entertaining/informative?	

Descriptive writing: Using the success criteria for descriptive writing, create text entitled '*The Professor's Room*' and '*The Artist's Room*' – first imagine what these characters might have in their rooms.

The Professor's Room

The Artist's Room

Project 4 – What makes good writing?

Style:
Do ambitious vocabulary and phrases, in a variety of sentence types with a range of punctuation, keep the reader engaged?

Content:
Is relevant information included that is based on good ideas?

Genre:
Have I understood what makes good for the specific genre? Have I fulfilled the purpose of the writing to entertain, inform or persuade?

Organisation:
Do ideas logically link to other ideas, with the support of relevant openers/connectives, in same subject paragraphs?

Speed:
Is the task satisfactorily completed?

Presentation:
Is the text legible and appropriately laid out?

Cut out these features of good writing and decide which is the most significant, placing this at the top of the pyramid and the least important at the bottom. If you think they have equal significance put them in one horizontal line.

Assessing narrative: The Battle to find Dr Joseph

Success criteria for 'what makes good writing'	Commentary/examples
Does the text involve good ideas?	
Is ambitious vocabulary used?	
Are ambitious phrases used?	
Are sentences varied?	
Is punctuation used accurately?	
Is text organised in paragraphs?	
Do ideas logically link?	
Do a range of sentence openers support text flow?	
Is enough relevant information included?	
Success criteria for 'what makes good story writing'	**Commentary/examples**
Does the narrative start with action?	
Is the main character introduced quickly?	
Is the setting introduced quickly?	
Is the dilemma introduced quickly?	
Does the narrative use cliffhangers?	
Is suspense successfully built up?	
Does the narrative maintain the reader's interest?	
Does the main character develop?	
Does the action build to a satisfactory resolution that links to previous action?	
Does the narrative entertain, inform or persuade?	
Would you recommend the story to others?	
How would you improve this narrative?	

Writing an entertaining narrative – complete this narrative, The Apprentice

The King's Room

The King looked at the boy quizzically. "So, you're Tarik. You're not what I was expecting and yet you come highly recommended. Tarik, you must reach the Clock-maker's room by noon, after going through the rooms of the Entertainer, the Professor and the Artist. You only have twenty-four minutes. In each room there will be a challenge for you to overcome, against all odds. Should you complete the mission in time and give me an answer to my question, you will become my worthy apprentice."

"What is the question, Sir?" asked Tarik.

The King smiled slightly, "If you are the one, I do not need to tell you," answered the King, mysteriously.

The Entertainer's Room

A sweet, strawberry scent dominated the Entertainer's room and small and large red dots adorned the stark white plastic floor, walls and ceiling. As the door closed behind Tarik, there was no obvious way out because the inside of the door was decorated to merge in. Tarik was overcome by a bizarre urge to laugh, but he did not have the time and so he didn't. However, as he sat down on a red lip Daliesque sofa, laughter and vibrations emanated from this smiling piece of furniture. Next to Tarik was a red and white party trumpet. As the laughter subsided, he blew into the plastic top of the instrument and instead of the anticipated coarse note, out came the eight magical opening beats of Beethoven's Fifth Symphony. Tarik blew it again and was surprised by an urgent, though friendly whisper, "Press the red button."

Tarik observed the room. Besides the sofa, the trumpet and him, there was nothing else there. So… the red button must be one of the red dots. But, there were hundreds of red dots and none of them appeared to be protruding. Quickly, Tarik pushed the sofa to one side and lay down on the floor. He stretched out his arms above his head and began to roll the length of the room. Nothing interrupted him. So, he then put his back against the wall and slid along it (again with arms stretched out above him) until he abruptly stopped. Sticking out from the wall was a domed red button. He was about to push it, but luckily he felt something resting on his right ear – a rolled up piece of paper, which when unrolled, held a vital clue:

Press it once and your world falls apart,
Press it correctly and you will depart.
Be infinitely wise!

The Fifth Symphony came to mind and so he began to press the button five times, but then he considered the eight opening beats that he had heard. Of course: '8' rotated ninety degrees became the sign for infinity – *Be infinitely wise!* He continued pressing the button and on the eighth push, a spontaneous sharp click accompanied the release of a camouflaged door in the wall opposite to where he had originally entered. Through this doorway, Tarik could see what was obviously the Professor's Room.

The Professor's Room

The Artist's Room

The Clock-maker's Room

Assessing narrative: The Apprentice

Use the success criteria to review and edit your own narrative writing.

Success criteria for 'what makes good writing'	Commentary/examples
Does the text involve good ideas?	
Is ambitious vocabulary used?	
Are ambitious phrases used?	
Are sentences varied?	
Is punctuation used accurately?	
Is text organised in paragraphs?	
Do ideas logically link?	
Do a range of sentence openers support text flow?	
Is enough relevant information included?	
Success criteria for 'what makes good story writing'	**Commentary/examples**
Does the narrative start with action?	
Is the main character introduced quickly?	
Is the setting introduced quickly?	
Is the dilemma introduced quickly?	
Does the narrative use cliffhangers?	
Is suspense successfully built up?	
Does the narrative maintain the reader's interest?	
Does the main character develop?	
Does the action build to a satisfactory resolution that links to previous action?	
Does the narrative entertain, inform or persuade?	
Would you recommend the story to others?	
How would you improve this narrative?	

Project 5 – Instructions text

Useful vocabulary for directions

Prepositions (usually precede a noun or pronoun to indicate temporal, spatial or logical connections): *across, along, amongst, around, before, behind, below, beneath, beside, between, beyond, by, down, following, during, following, inside, into, near, next, opposite, outside, over, past, round, through, towards, under, underneath, until, up, via, with, without*

Connectives (can be conjunctions when they link clauses in the same sentence or they can link sentences or paragraphs together as connecting adverbs): *alternatively, although, anyway, besides, consequently, eventually, finally, firstly, furthermore, however, indeed, lastly, meanwhile, nevertheless, nonetheless, notwithstanding, suddenly, then, therefore*

Co-ordinating conjunctions (join two main clauses in a compound sentence): *and, but, for, or, so yet*

Subordinating conjunctions (join an idea with a dependent idea in a sentence): *after, although, as, because, before, even though, if, once, that, since, until, when, while, who*

Correlative conjunctions (join balanced ideas with pairs of words in a sentence): *both… and, either… or, neither… nor, not only… but also, whether… or*

Adjectives (describe nouns or pronouns): *aggressive, ancient, archaic, battered, bumpy, crooked, crowded, dangerous, dank, dark, difficult, discordant, distinct, elegant, empty, flaky, fragile, frail, gloomy, grotesque, heavy, hollow, icy, intimidating, melodic, metallic, microscopic, misty, numerous, overgrown, precious, prickly, rapid, restless, resonant, shallow, shrill, slippery, smooth, steep, swift, thundering*

Nouns (name of a person, animal, place, thing or idea): *caves, city, cove, creature, echo, foliage, forest, guards, mirror, ocean, river, lake, mountain, palace, path, sky, track, valley, village, villagers, warrior*

Verbs (words that indicate an action or a state of being): *advance, amble, appreciate, ascend, calculate, climb, defeat, descend, hasten, hover, hurry, meander, overcome, progress, resist, stoop, trample*

Adverbs (describe verbs): *cautiously, courageously, discreetly, faithfully, ferociously, frequently, gently, instinctively, intelligently, leisurely, ominously, silently, spontaneously, stoically, swiftly, vivaciously*

Play the 'Alphabet Game' and see how many letters of the alphabet start vocabulary for a word type, such as adjectives, adverbs or connectives. For example: *anxious, brutal, creative, dangerous, excited, friendly…*

Complete the instructional text below, for how to reach Dr Joseph, using some of the above vocabulary. Include some imaginary creatures.

When the prison guard is sleeping, sneak out of the Royal Dungeons, quietly. Scale the high perimeter wall of the Palace, dropping lightly on to Homage Hill. Be careful of the spiteful thorns and Mr Jack, the half-human and half-pig, who is very grumpy if woken.

Information text: Non-chronological report on Oliver Island

Use the success criteria for non-chronological report writing to annotate a commentary for the first two paragraphs about Oliver Island before completing the report, with such items as major landmarks, flora and fauna, working lives, leisure time and culture. Write a short final paragraph that either sums up an overall view of Oliver Island or looks forward to the future of Oliver Island.

- ❑ **Vocabulary:** Use ambitious, formal and technical vocabulary that suits the topic. Use mostly present tense, unless past tense is required for historical information or future tense is required to look forward.

- ❑ **Sentences:** Use topic sentences (sentences that show the subject and direction of the paragraph) to start each paragraph, so that you know what each paragraph is about. Use a range of sentences, including compound and complex sentences in order that more information is provided in a succinct and effective fashion.

- ❑ **Paragraphs:** Do not write titles down for each paragraph, but know what the subject is for each paragraph, so that you group together the same sort of information. Cover relevant aspects of what/who, where, when, why and/or how. Have a final paragraph that looks forward.

- ❑ **Content:** Make interesting information sound factual.

Oliver Island

Oliver Island is a self-sufficient island to the south of New Zealand. Inhabited by humans since the seventeenth century, it has had its own monarch since 1850 and today it has a population of twelve thousand.

Five monarchs have reigned over the people of Oliver Island, all of them descendants of Oliver James who was the first settler on the island in 1695. In 1850, Charles Edward James was inaugurated as the first monarch, by popular vote of the islanders to give the James' family royal status. In response to this honour, Charles Edward created the magnificent walled Royal City, which originally housed the whole population and protected them from the wild animals that also inhabited the island. He is further known for having established the Scholars' District, with a university and an education for every island child. In 1895, Charles Edward died in a tragic hunting accident and his eldest son, Henry Arthur, was welcomed as the ruler of the islanders. A talented artist, Henry Arthur created the Royal Pottery that still exports its distinct fauna decorated pots around the World today. Henry Arthur's youngest son, Samuel, emerged as the island's third monarch in 1936, as his father had outlived his siblings. He abdicated in 1950, after an uprising against his unpopular and harsh taxes and he died mysteriously, while sailing. His unhappy ghost is said to roam the streets of the Royal City. Having restored harmony on the island, King Oliver (Samuel's only heir) reigned for fifty years. In the year 2000, Matlock, Oliver's eldest son) was crowned monarch. Unusually, he has shared the governing of the Island with his twin brother, Riley, since 2005, following the threat of civil war. Today, the twins are probably the most popular royals in the history of Oliver Island, having established reforms that have improved the welfare of all its citizens.

Project 6 – Persuasive text: names and slogans

A product, brand or campaign can be reflected by its name. A slogan is a phrase used at the end of adverts to make a product, brand or campaign memorable and appealing. Slogans sometimes use questions, superlatives, puns, alliteration or rhyme. Create names and slogans for these new products, brands or campaigns.

Product, brand or campaign name	Information	Slogan and analysis
Eighty	A fast-food chain that only sells tasty, healthy international food from eighty different countries	*Zest in a jiffy* (zest is a pun as it means exciting, enjoyable, citrus peel and a piquant flavour, while 'in a jiffy' means imminently and has a suggestion of lemons)
Getting to know you	A campaign to persuade everyone to care about everyone else in the community for one day	*What will you do?* (Makes the audience responsible and part of this campaign by getting them to think what they could do for their own community)
	A healthy, sparkling fruit cocktail drink	
	A new brand of sportswear	
	A campaign to educate adolescents so that they never smoke	

Analysing a radio advert to persuade visitors to the Oliver Island Museum

It is important to understand the purpose of any writing. In writing an advert to persuade any age group to visit the Oliver Island Museum, the overall assessment of whether the text is successful is whether or not it fulfils the aim of the writing, that is: would it persuade anyone to visit the Oliver Island Museum when read out?

Use the grid below to analyse the advert for the Oliver Island Museum

Fancy an exhilarating and memorable day out for all the family? Then come on down to the Oliver Island Museum.

❏ *Enjoy an invigorating ride into history with the time machine and meet the people of yesteryear.*

❏ *Participate in a thrilling holographic adventure to escape the wild animals of the past.*

❏ *Create stunning pottery decorated with animals the Island way.*

❏ *Produce a rousing short film about islanders in our hi-tech studios for our film theatre shows.*

❏ *Test out your scientific know-how with Professor Bubble and save the island from ruin in our inspiring hands-on Science lab.*

❏ *Taste the delicious flavours of international cuisine in the Oliver Café or The King's Rooms Restaurant*

Bursting to the walls with many explosive rides and breathtaking experiences, the Museum is for you!

So come on down to the Oliver Island Museum, The Royal Drive, Scholars' District. Open Mondays to Saturdays inclusive, 9.00am to 5.00pm. Check it out at OliverIslandMuseum.com.

At Oliver Island Museum wonders never cease!

What lead question is used?	
What is the product name?	
How is the product described to show its benefits?	
What positive adjectives are used to describe the product?	
What opinion is made to sound like fact?	
What other crucial information is included?	
What snappy slogan is used?	
How is the advert organised?	
Is the advert persuasive and to whom?	

Oliver Island Museum – analysis of the advert

How well did you analyse the advert?

What lead question is used?	Fancy an exhilarating and memorable day out for all the family?
What is the product name?	Then come on down to the Oliver Island Museum.
How is the product described to show its benefits?	❏ Enjoy an invigorating ride into history with the time machine and meet the people of yesteryear. ❏ Participate in a thrilling holographic adventure to escape the wild animals of the past. ❏ Create stunning pottery decorated with animals the Island way. ❏ Produce a rousing short film about islanders in our hi-tech studios for our film theatre shows. ❏ Test out your scientific know-how with Professor Bubble and save the island from ruin in our inspiring hands-on Science lab. ❏ Taste the delicious flavours of international cuisine in the Oliver Café or The King's Rooms Restaurant. Bursting to the walls with many explosive rides and breathtaking experiences, the Museum is for you!
What positive adjectives are used to describe the product?	Exhilarating, memorable, invigorating, thrilling, stunning, rousing, inspiring, delicious, explosive, breathtaking
What opinion is made to sound like fact?	Bursting to the walls with many explosive rides and breathtaking experiences, the Museum is for you!
What other crucial information is included?	So come on down to the Oliver Island Museum, The Royal Drive, Scholars' District. Open Mondays to Saturdays inclusive, 9.00am to 5.00pm. Check it out at OliverIslandMuseum.com
What snappy slogan is used?	At Oliver Island Museum wonders never cease!
How is the advert organised?	Question, name, benefits, directions, slogan. The benefits are easy to identify as they are set out with bullet points.
Is the advert persuasive and to whom?	The content and the language are used to persuade visitors of all ages.

Does the advert fulfil the general success criteria for writing well?

Success criteria	Analysis with reference to the advert
Content: Is relevant information included that is based on good ideas?	
Style: Do ambitious vocabulary and phrases, in a variety of sentence types, with a range of punctuation, keep the reader engaged?	
Organisation: Do ideas logically link to other ideas, with the support of relevant openers/connectives in same subject paragraphs?	
Genre: Is there an understanding of what makes good for the specific genre? Is the aim of the writing to entertain, inform or persuade fulfilled?	
Presentation: Is the text legible and appropriately laid out?	
Speed: Is the task satisfactorily completed?	

Writing a radio advert to persuade anyone to visit the Royal Palace, Oliver Island

Write a radio advert that would persuade anyone of any age group to visit the Royal Palace, Oliver Island. First, consider what the Palace can offer a visitor. Then, plan your advert in the grid before you write out your text that would be read out on radio. Continue to consider the success criteria in order to assess and develop your advert.

What lead question is used?	
What is the product name?	
How is the product described to show its benefits?	
What positive adjectives are used to describe the product?	
What opinion is made to sound like fact?	
What other crucial information is included?	
What snappy slogan is used?	
How is the advert organised?	
Is the advert persuasive and to whom?	

A radio advert for the Royal Palace, Oliver Island.